Missing
Mom
Pieces

Christy Lawler

ISBN 978-1-64416-888-2 (paperback)
ISBN 978-1-64416-951-3 (hardcover)
ISBN 978-1-64416-889-9 (digital)

Christian Faith Publishing, Inc.
832 Park Avenue
Meadville, PA 16335
www.christianfaithpublishing.com

Printed in the United States of America

I heard this song and have played it often, I realized it is me.

> Here I am God,
> Arms wide open
> Pouring out my life gracefully broken
> My heart stands in awe of Your name
> Your mighty love stands strong to the end
> You will fulfill Your purpose for me
> You won't forsake me
> You will be with me
> Here I am God,
> Arms wide open
> Pouring out my life gracefully broken
> Holding nothing back
> I surrender
> I surrender
> I surrender . . .

Father God, I lift the reader of this book up to you! May they find the peace that You offer, along with love, forgiveness, understanding, and wisdom. Those things You offer so freely to all of us with one word, *salvation*. I pray they find those pieces of themselves that have been missing, lost, or just need renewed. May they look at the "moms" in their lives a little differently with each page they read. Work in my heart as I go on this journey, this journey to collect and put together all my "missing Mom pieces."

> Have I not commanded you? Be strong and cou-
> rageous. Do not be afraid; do not be discouraged,

3

for the Lord your God will be with you wherever
you go. (Joshua 1:9)

Trust in the Lord with all your heart and lean not
on your own understand; in all your ways submit to him, and he will make your paths straight.
(Proverbs 3:5–6, NIV)

Trust in the Lord with all your heart; do not
depend on your own understanding. Seek his
will in all you do, and he will show you which
path to take. (Proverbs 3:5–6, NLT)

So that is why I do this, to find the missing pieces and heal at
least part of it. It's also a way to fight for those that couldn't fight for
themselves. And maybe, it's giving a voice where none were heard
before.

I couldn't fight for myself as a child, and I didn't have a voice
loud enough or strong enough to move mountains or stop people
from hurting me or my siblings. I believe my mother, for a time, was
in the same position as me. I would like you to read this but not for
a pity, not for sympathy, but instead to know where I was and where
I am now. Also to know that someone gets it a little bit. And you are
not alone. Even as I write this, I am not alone. God is always with me!

There might be times we rabbit trail, but we won't get lost. We
will find our way back quickly, I hope. And then, there are times I
joke around. Maybe at the keyboard, I don't want to let the tears fall
or emotions run high.

So if I step off the trail a moment, I promise to come back and
continue down the path we were taking. Don't be afraid to get angry
with me if you think I am too harsh. I can handle it. Just don't give
up on me! I want to show you there is hope on how to get your missing pieces found and possibly put back together, maybe not how they
were but even a little better. And as we travel, this rout shows you
who is great at fixing the messes in our lives with possible messages
for others later.

In this book, each of the sections start with a question I have asked others about their mother figures. They are questions God laid on my heart as this book idea grew. Some sections may be long or shorter, depending on how I responded myself to them. My purpose for this was to live through others that had a good relationship with their moms. But as the idea grew and people responded to the questionnaire, I found I wanted to heal and help others heal from the wounds in their hearts, to give hope that healing can come if they wanted it. Maybe the emotional scars would look a little less like a loss and more like a victory in what you had come through. So even through this writing, not only do I get to share a part of my story but parts of others as well. I get to speak for those afraid to speak out loud of the pains they had. I am blessed to know others have trusted me enough with the secrets or hurts they keep hidden. Also those that have blessed me with great stories of moms who were able to give the love they did.

I want to tell you that none of this is meant to hurt my mother or anyone in her family. Some things may come off as mean or unchristian-like, that's not my intentions. Even now, I apologize for things I say or justify why I am doing this.

I spoke to someone I trust (very tough sometimes), and I was willing to listen to their council (again, very difficult) on this project. As I did that, I had a lot of questions.

This is some of what I said or asked:

"I have to answer these questions as well, how will I do that? How much of me goes into this? How much of 'the walls' come down to look into my life? Is it a complete secret?"

"No, then the whole process is a waste of time. I would not be doing anything worthwhile without skin in the game or words on the pages!"

His response: "We cannot hide from truth, but God will heal us so we can speak the truth in love." (E.J. 1/23/2017)

So that is what I want to do. Will you join me? If it's hard at times because of pain you have, it's going to be okay. Just put it down and come back when you are ready. That's what I have had to do, many, many times, again and again. And it really is okay, and I mean that as I can continue on my own time and ability. So continue on your time and your ability. If things become difficult for you, will you seek someone out that you trust to help you process what comes up, maybe even a professional? It will help in the bigger picture of healing. As you read this, you may feel I am talking directly to you. As if you and I are sitting at my table or in the sunroom, enjoying a cup of coffee or tea just chatting about life. I want to speak to you as an individual; you are important to me. How can you be important to me? Because somewhere in your life, someone has possibly said something that made your heart hurt, made you feel a little more insecure than you thought. Not that we can't take it, but it still might hurt. I believe our hurts and happiness in life help make us who we are, and sometimes, strength comes from enduring pain. But isn't it hard being strong all the time? I have learned I don't have to, but God will. I pray that I have placed verses of God's Word in the right place at the right time for you. I want your heart not to hurt as badly or not at all. So you see you are important to me.

You will have the chance to answer each chapter question yourself in the space provided. You may even need to write your answers on a separate sheet of paper if it is long. May I ask that you be honest with yourself because that is where you start to heal? You might want to highlight any Scripture that speaks to you.

If you have a different version other than what I have used, look it up and compare so you are comfortable with them.

Are you ready?

Let's do this!

Chapter 1

What Was the Most Important Thing Your Mother Figure Taught You?

I'm not sure how you feel, but I think life gets tough sometimes. I'm sure you get that. If you are reading this and breathing, you know what I mean. I believe struggles come in all forms and situations. Though I will admit, I never saw myself writing about mothers as being a rough experience or how some may not get it right. Yes, I include myself in that statement. I know I have messed up in this area many times. As I watch my girls become moms, I don't want them to feel this way. I don't want them to sit back and say, "Wow, she really messed it all up!" I must own my part and heal from the damage of my own mother missing the mark with me. So I need to go back another generation for a moment.

I remember how my grandmother was, my mother's mom. I can still see her cooking or doing tri-chem (that's a type of paint). From what I recall, my grandmother was capable of a lot of things. She cooked, baked (best chocolate pie ever), sewed, painted, and canned (one reason I can't stand cats or green beans. LOL). She cleaned the house, took care of my grandfather, and sometimes watched the grandchildren. She bowled on a team every week, and she went to church. I know where she went bowling, but I have no idea where she attended services. I just know she talked about it like it was just another thing she did during her week of activities. I don't remember my grandfather ever going with her, and she never took any of the grandchildren that I can remember. She even taught me how to paint. She taught her daughters how to paint and sew and cook, and those things were needed to take care of themselves and a family. So why not teach some of the other most important things?

My point about what my grandmother did is this. At what age did she teach my mother that it was okay to put up with abuse and neglect? To turn her back on her kids and not grow up? To be responsible for the lives she brought into this world? To put a male, not a man, because men don't do these things to people they say they love, but put a male that clearly was unsafe in her life or children's lives? When was she taught that? Was it in "how to put up with being treated like a dirty doormat and a punching bag 101?" I never saw her teach my mother that, but she learned it from someone. What I also never saw was my grandmother teaching my mom how to stop it. If she was not the one who taught, she also was the one who stood by and watched and didn't do a whole lot. Kind of like the attitude of today, "I don't want to get involved."

Unfortunately, that dirty doormat and punching bag 101 classes has been taken by many, many people. I took that class, too, multiple times. Of course, it started at home with my parents. Always got an A-plus for attendance; maybe that's why I was a good student into my adult life.

As I type this out, I feel the bitterness and anger come rushing in; my face is getting hot. It's the second time today I have felt that way. Yes, same subject.

The conversation with my husband was about all the things in this world you need a license for. A license is needed for driving, fishing, hunting, being a doctor, lawyer, foster parenting. I'm sure you can think of others as well. Parenting your own child is not one of them. I guess being responsible for another life is not that important if they are your own. If we did need to be licensed as parents, I wouldn't have passed the test right away either. So all the things we learn or do not learn, we get to pass on to our children!

So I think this is a great time to introduce a few really good verses.

> Likewise, teach the older women to be reverent in
> the way they live, not to be slanderers or addicted

8

> to much wine, but to teach what is good. Then they can urge the younger women to love their husbands and children, to be self-controlled and pure, to be busy at home, to be kind, and to be subject to their husbands, so that no one will malign (to say evil things about) the Word of God. (Titus 2:3–5, NIV)

Before anyone gets upset, I'm not saying be home, barefoot, pregnant, never drink, and do everything your husband says. These few verses are a direct command for generations before us to get it, learn, and pass it on to the younger generations. To get it right so these tragic things don't continue to plague the next generation. In this day and age, that's a hard one. First of all, there are a lot of families that don't have a strong man that is the spiritual leader in their homes. I was a single parent for a while. It's tough doing it on your own. But families need that. I never realized how much until Jesus became my Savior. But we will save the men being leaders for another time. Because if you are a single mom, you have to be everything! As a mom, in general, you need to teach what is right and good and protect. I know somewhere, my grandmother, her mother, and so on, dropped the ball so hard I felt the outcome. And if I felt the outcome, so did my mother, my siblings, and my children, until now.

This doesn't mean I will be perfect from this day forward. What it looks like is I will try so hard and seek out every way I can to get it close to wonderful.

> Wonderful: causing wonder, marvelous, very good or fine.

I think that's a nice place to start.

I was sitting here trying to think what was the most important thing my mother taught me? I have gone back and forth on many things. Yet, none of those items are the most important. So I dig a little deeper, deeper, deeper, and finally, I find the strength to say, how not to be like her forever. Those that know me will say, "You are nothing like your mother!" But I was, at many points in my life. I learned how to turn a blind eye to the truth in my face. I learned how not to grow up and take care of my children when they were little. I learned how to choose drugs, alcohol, sex, and males before them. I learned how not to protect them in the beginning. I learned how not to choose them over my wants and selfish ways. I learned how not to take care of myself when it came to my mental well-being. I learned how to look at myself in the mirror and see nothing good, nothing positive.

How to lie to people and say everything is great, he didn't mean it, it was my fault, if I had done things differently. I learned to blame others if they said I had a problem with drugs or just deny it all together. I learned how to hide a depression diagnosis for fear of being abandoned. I learned anger is my best emotion. I learned that if I didn't acknowledge what was wrong, I didn't have to work to fix it. I learned how to think I am unworthy, unworthy of love, compassion, being protected. I learned how to not think for myself, to be controlled, to be used, to feel dirty. Maybe that no amount of showering was to wash the filth from myself I felt, maybe.

Basically, I deserved everything I ever got. She taught me that. Those are things I learned as a child to carry with me as tools for living life. Actually, I was just life existing.

I have heard some of those words be spoken by her. I saw the scars she carried on the outside. And I watched her struggle from the ones on the inside. Do you know when you watch someone being beat on, and constantly beat down verbally, emotionally, and physically that you are actually watching a part of them die?

So growing up, we were watching her die? We watched her physically fight for her life as well as emotionally. Am I saying she taught me how to die a little? Yes, I believe I am. Or is that too harsh? Whether it is too harsh or not, it's truth. There is a lot of truth that we will share with each other here. And it's okay. It's safe to do this.

Am I trying to convince you or me? Me. It's going to be okay; it is safe. It has to be to continue this journey. Safe doesn't mean it won't be difficult.

"I sought the Lord, and he answered me; he delivered me from all my fears" (Psalm 34:4).

Why that verse? Why that short, very powerful verse? Because there is pain peeling back the layers and layers of memories and scars, and it can cause some fear. It's the unknown of others actions. It's the pain of reality that if I choose not to be like her, I have to speak it. I have to open up the old wounds the right way so they get air and cleaned out properly and then medication to heal the correct way. It has to get to the point where a word or phrase won't make me want to hide. I have to allow God to take the chains that have bound me with such great frustration and pain for so long be busted for good! I need to make sure the chains are only fragments, better yet just dust, with no chance of becoming whole again and grabbing my children any further or my grandchildren at all. It's time to heal to protect them from some of the life choices I lived or taught.

So I have said it was not to be like her for forever. This really isn't meant to bash her. It is to teach the younger ones how not to be. It's to remind me people change, people live what they know, but they really can change if they want to and fight for it. It doesn't have to be a fake it till ya make it thing. It's so another young girl or woman can hold her head up and stop carrying a yoke around her neck with shame, guilt, and all the other pains she has. Being forever connected with only one job to be done, being in pain every single day. They need someone to invest time in them with nothing in return, except to see them get it right.

It's very sad she wasn't taught how important she was and that her voice should be heard. That she should be respected for more than a baby factory or a punching bag or a maid. That the one she would marry would love only her. That she would be cherished by him. What about the fact she was worth fighting for? That she was smart and beautiful, and she was beautiful. I saw her high school picture, and it was the first time I saw her "alive." Her smile was so real in that picture. I don't think there were many times I saw that in life with her. So I wonder how many years it took to break that life down to merely a shell. How many people used her and forgot she was a beautiful baby, a funny toddler, a little girl who was curious?

She was a teenager, looking to find her place in this world, a woman who wanted to be loved and respected. She was a woman who had none of that, until maybe right this moment.

In this moment that feels like a tiny window with a tiny opening, giving only the smallest amount of love. It should be so much more, I'm trying.

Her mother didn't fight for her. I believe she had one brother fight for her, he was awesome. He was a navy man with honor. He was my hero as a child, and he still is! He went home to be with Jesus years ago, and I miss him so much. (I can still recall the last face-to-face conversation I had with him and the last phone call we had right before he died. Dance with Jesus, Uncle, dance with Jesus!)

Her own father did not stand up for her. When my father would beat her and she would call her father, who I was told was a city cop, he always sent her back. It was always, "Her choice, I don't want to upset her or take the kids' father away." Please, he was a coward who hid behind a badge, if he really carried one. No wonder I had no respect for police officers growing up. I used to think it was because they always took my "daddy" away. Maybe he couldn't handle what the badge meant. I believe he ended up working for the city in the water or sewer department. I don't know why he changed jobs. Maybe he worked long enough to retire. I don't know. I know I am being hard on him, but it's how I saw it. I'm sure that my brothers, sisters, and other family might see it differently. And that difference, well I almost let it stop me from writing. I was having fear of upsetting aunts, uncles, cousins, or siblings that loved and respected him. But as I said earlier, it is how I saw it.

In the eyes of children, they may all see it very differently. As an adult, I feel like a lot of what I saw or believed as a child was true. We can't ask him now because he is gone. I loved him growing up, I think. I wanted too, so from what I knew of love, I guess I did. I thought he didn't love me. When we would get to their house, I would run and put my arms around his leg or waist, depending on how high I was. And I would get the same reaction all the time: a pat on the head or back and a hello with an awkward laugh, almost as if uncomfortable, then nothing. He used to hit the cats with a rolled up newspaper; I always waited for him to use it on me. He was always so serious, no laughing at the table, no talking. How can you have ten kids eating together with no noise? But that's what we were to him, noise. It wasn't until I was much older that I knew my grandfather loved us; he just couldn't handle my father. He did finally tell me he loved me. Even though he said he loved me, it isn't enough to respect him. Even though he couldn't do something about my father, someone else on the force could have.

My only daughter at the time, who was four, and I went back to Oregon for a summer. Before we left for Pennsylvania, he hugged me and said I love you. He even hugged my daughter and gave her a brown bear. I think she broke him while we were there. Every morning, she would go hug him and any time before we left that house. She would sit on his lap and just talk his ear off. I saw him smile. And I thought that's what it looked like to see him smile. He had no choice but to break. Maybe he saw me? Maybe it was there that his heart broke for what he had not done for his daughter or his granddaughter, but looking at his great granddaughter, maybe she melted the coldness away. I want to believe that God had something to do with that coldness going away too. He is gone now, so that is what I will hang on to.

Before I take any more side roads, I need to get back to the most important thing she taught me. Somewhere deep down, I love her. Maybe because I am supposed to, maybe because God says love her. I won't lie; it's very difficult, painful, and sometimes downright unbelievable to want to love her, to like her. Sometimes, I think I need to keep my heart hard about her to protect myself. Protection from wanting a mother, yet knowing it won't ever happen. When I catch myself doing that, I find my heart hardens to the life around me. I cry out to God.

How do you walk away from your daughter being beaten with a wet leather belt? Did I lie to him? Yes. Did I deserve a punishment? Yes. She was afraid of her second husband (my father)? She had already taken so much, and maybe she felt she didn't earn this one. I know at first she wanted to come in and save me. But at the only attempt at a step over the metal strip came a threat toward her.

"Come over that line and you will get it as well as her but worse!" I watched her walk away, saying "You're not worth it." I was in second grade. Can you imagine the weight of that lesson right there? The very impact those four words had on me then, and even now.

So if I wasn't worth fighting for then, how about later, or in the future? Over and over again, she proved how true that statement was, how real it became in my life. How ugly of a truth it was. How many times would she stay in her room "sleeping" so my father could molest me? How many times would she get mad at me when he took me fishing? It wasn't my fault he never took her. I waited and waited for her to say she was going. Maybe she was mad because she knew what was happening and thought it was my fault. I did something to deserve the abuse. But the look she would always give me is the look she gave when he and other woman would "hang out." The look as if she was losing him to someone else, again. *Hello!* I was her daughter, not some strange woman she saw as competition! I was a child! I only went to protect others. If he took me, no one else was getting abused, threatened, or hurt. I thought I was protecting them. I couldn't. Does that mean I asked to be abused or I wanted it? *No!* I was a child! I thought I could be brave one day and stand up to him and then it would stop. And he would be gone or he would be a good dad. And then she would love me. I didn't. I couldn't. She didn't know how.

How could she love something when she wasn't shown love? Or didn't want it. I found out a few years ago, after one of her strokes, how she really felt about me. She was well enough to talk, and she still had her speech, her memory. It was only her walking and griping and guard that were damaged. Her guard? Yes, the part of her brain where she kept the darkest of secrets hidden from everyone. It was as if a young child was telling on someone. That's sort of what she did. We talked about the pictures in her wallet, pictures of the oldest child, none. Pictures of the second child, there were many. Pictures of the third child, there were many. Pictures of the fourth child, me, there were none. Pictures of the fifth child, there were a few. My sister and I that where there (the second child) flew to see her. I had not seen her in twenty plus years. The big sis had not seen her in thirty plus, nor spoke to her for that many.

We then talked about traits we shared. Our mother and my sister made fun of me for how the middle toe on each foot look like my middle fingers, longer than the rest. My sister said, "How come I can't turn my wrist all the way over like my other?" Palms up flat, I believe her right hand only goes half to three quarters over.

Like a child, our mother said, "Did you hurt it when you were little? You know, like break it?" *Wow*! She knew what happened. She used to grab my sister's hand and twist at the wrist to make her listen. Did she break my sister's wrist and not tell anyone or get it fixed? If you could have seen her face and reaction, you would say yes she did.

Seeing it in print, it has to sink in a minute or five. I know we were going to possibly say goodbye. I had no idea what to expect. Instead, we were going to find out things we had never known. Maybe I want to unknow. I wish we could pick and choose the things to un-know in our lives. So, yes, off the trail a bit. There is a big boulder in the way that needs to be removed. Like the last one we tossed off the trail, this, too, is a little tough. One of us said something about her nickname, Penny. She got this weird look on her face and said, "Penny is gone, I don't like her, and I don't like being called by that name." Can you picture the look my sis shot me? Like did you just hear that? Does our mother have multiple personalities? Christy! Did you hear that? If I can say that is what she said in that one look, yes she did.

Basically, what happened was "Penny" was a scrapper, she was tough and could tolerate tons. When life was like that, chaos, turmoil, and trouble, Penny was around. She could be a smart butt and laugh. When life was too difficult or hurt too much, she was there. One night, my father was "ornery" as she put it. And then she had me. My father raped my mother. All I could hear was you are only here because that sick person took advantage of a woman and hurt her. You are the result of pain. So, all of this to say why there were no pictures of me in her belongings. Finally, there is a reason why she didn't like me or protect me. Why look at something every day that brought memories of pain? Why help that child from hurting when she had to look at that child every day and hurt anyway? I was in her presence because of a painful event in her life. She simply didn't deserve another painful moment where I was concerned. So I was a constant reminder of pain, so why not get mad when he wanted me around and not her? No wonder she could not see me as her child but yet another hurt my father brought to her life.

If I listen to this truth and not God's truth, I miss something very important. One of my girls sent this scripture, this truth to me shortly after my mother's memories became known.

> But even before I was born, God chose me and called me by his marvelous grace. (Galatians 1:15, NLT)

> For you created my inmost being; you knit me together in my mother's womb. I praise you because I am fearfully and wonderfully made; your works are wonderful, I know that full well. (Psalm 139:13–14)

So I choose to hold that truth about why I am here. I am not the product of a rape. I am here because God loved me so much; He wanted me! He gave me life! As much as I love the last truth, I am sorry, we must continue.

When there is no more fight in you and things are never going to get better, you just give in. Years of abuse and hate and being treated as if you are owned and not married, who wouldn't want left alone? She knew she couldn't make him change. She knew about all of them, the other woman, the other girls. The runaway girl, he took somewhere. I was actually afraid for that one. She was a young African American. And he was a racist pig. We never saw her again once the two of them left the house. My mother stayed in her room until he got back hours later. I don't even remember her name. I'm sorry I forget her name. She was someone's daughter, grandchild, maybe sister, someone's friend. She was someone who mattered. I'm sorry he hurt you. I'm sorry my mother didn't protect you. I couldn't. We couldn't; we didn't know how. We couldn't tell anyone because we were always prisoners in his hell. I'm so sorry.

It makes me wonder how many victims there were as she turned away from us. I'm not saying she made him do those things, but she sure in heck didn't protect me or anyone else from him. I feel like she couldn't. Like I said, we lived in the hell he created. So why am I so mad if I believe she really didn't know how or couldn't?

You would think that at some point, to look into her children's eyes, she would see a glimpse of her own childhood. That maybe she would scrap with someone to protect us, to save us. Again, maybe she couldn't. Then again, what example of a mom fighting for her child did she ever see? I understand in the 60's and 70's, you just didn't go against your spouse because they were in charge. Submitting was part of her job description. Domestic violence was not in the everyday vocabulary. Maybe she didn't know how. Maybe she was too tired and didn't want to chance another fight for her own safety. Maybe, just maybe, she just didn't want to. I have and would again go against someone for my children's well-being. I think if you ask my girls, they would say yes, she will fight for me. If they speak that at least once, then I am not like her forever.

I am sure there are some that will not be happy with these words in print. Some may look at me and think I am not being a very good Christian or think I will bring embarrassment to my family for speaking of things that are so personal and private. Some may think I am being too hard on her. That she did what she could because of where she was in her life. If I hang on to that fear of people's opinions or someone in her family or any of the siblings being mad at me for my words, then fear has won; the enemy would win, and there would be no heart mending here. Fear can be healthy and help in a situation. Or it can stop you in your tracks, to never move forward and learn and heal. I choose healing, and I want it for all of us.

On his arrival, Jesus found that Lazarus had already been in the tomb for four days. Bethany was less than two miles from Jerusalem, and many Jews had come to Martha and Mary to comfort them in the loss of their brother. When Martha heard that Jesus was coming, she went out to meet him, but Mary stayed at home. "Lord," Martha said to Jesus, "if you had been here, my brother would not have died. But I know that even now God will give you whatever you ask." Jesus said to her, "Your brother will rise again." Martha answered, "I know he will rise again in the resurrection at the last day." Jesus said to her, "I am the resurrection and the life, he who believes in me will live, even though he dies; and whoever lives and believes in me will never die. Do you believe this?" "Yes, Lord," she told him, "I believe that you are the Christ, the Son of God, who was to come into the world." And after she had said this, she went back and called her sister Mary aside. "The Teacher is here," she said, "and is asking for you." when Mary heard this, she got up quickly and went to the place where Martha had met him. When the Jews who had been with Mary in the house, comforting her, noticed how quickly she got up and went out, they followed her supposing she was going to the tomb to mourn there. When Mary reached the place where Jesus was and saw him, she fell at his feet and said, "Lord, if you had been here, my brother would not have died." When Jesus saw her weeping, and the Jews who had come along with her also weeping, he was deeply moved in spirit and troubled. "Where have you laid him?" he asked. "Come and see, Lord," they replied. Jesus wept. Then the Jews said, "See how he loved him!" But some of them said, "Could not he who opened the eyes of the blind man have kept this man from dying?"

Jesus, once more deeply moved, came to the tomb. It was a cave with a stone laid across the entrance. "Take away the stone," he said. "But,

Lord," said Martha, the sister of the dead man, "by this time there is a bad odor, for he has been there four days." Then Jesus said, "Did I not tell you that if you believed, you would see the glory of God?" So they took away the stone. Then Jesus looked up and said, "Father, I thank you that you have heard me. I knew that you always hear me, but I said this for the benefit of the people standing here, that they may believe that you sent me." When he had said this, Jesus called in a loud voice, "Lazarus, come out!" The dead man came out, his hands and feet wrapped with strips of linen and a cloth around his face. Jesus said to them, "Take off the grave clothes and let him go." (John 11:17–44)

So there are a few things with this passage. First, Jesus is the resurrection and the life. He is salvation for the lost, the hurting. He is Christ, the Son of God who came to this world to save us all. All who want His saving, it is free; we cannot earn it!

My second thought on this passage is He loves us so much! He knew Lazarus was going to live again. Even in knowing that, watching his friends Mary and Martha hurting, he felt that pain. He wept, He cried for them and their pain. So knowing that and I believe it true, how much does He love me? How much does my pain cause Him to weep? Even pain I have caused myself makes Him weep. Your pain makes him weep. The love He has for you is huge! If you don't know it, it's right there for you to grab. If you do know it but have fallen by the way side, stand up and grab his hand to help you back up. If you know and are walking, keep walking, but let Him guide you to those that need help up or acknowledgement of who He is. And don't forget to love on them!

Weep with them if you need to.

This is where we get to hear from others who wanted to talk about their mothers. As this book idea was growing, literally twenty-four hours after the thought, God blessed me with questions to ask others. So with the help of a very talented friend, we put together a questionnaire for others to share some of their stories, similar to what I said in the beginning. I feel it is important enough to repeat a little. In a lot of the questions, we actually had some of you responding the same way. So some chapters may seem to have more responses than others and that is why. I wanted to incorporate as many answers as possible because you took the time to answer, and I know it wasn't always easy. In some of the responses, you might see a number inside parenthesis that is the number of duplicate answers. They are also not in any particular order. We also must remember that these are things that have happened in others' lives, and we might not agree with what they have said. As far as Scripture, I have verified that all of it is correct.

This part is just as much healing for me as writing about my own mom. I get to live through others' words about what their mothers taught them, to see the good things they learned and get to pass on. And then there will be those that didn't have it so great. As I read them, my heart just hurt for the pain they had and some still have pain. I wanted to include them as well, so they knew they were not alone. I, too, have wept for many of you. So just as we share in joy and celebration with some, we can also feel the pain of the others and cry out to God on their behalf for healing.

Responses

What was the most important thing your mother taught you?

1. To love without judgment.
2. What not to be like.
3. Love and graciousness (I wish I would have put it in to practice more).
4. There were six nothing or blank answers.
5. To love my husband.
6. Self-preservation and what kind of person or mother not to be.
7. Having a sense of humor about things. Don't be too uptight about farts and burps.
8. Be yourself, be kind and always help others.
9. How to cook. How to become controlling.
10. Think before you speak and talk to your husband in private about matters that should not be discussed in front of children.
11. Responsibility.
12. Live what you preach.
13. Money isn't everything.
14. To always be true to yourself.
15. To give your kids room even when they are angry, and they will come around, just be kind until they do.
16. Never stop praying.
17. To work hard and not take things for granted.
18. To love God and put Him first.
19. Don't abuse my children.
20. How to make something out of nothing.
21. A good work ethic.
22. Boldness.
23. To see the good in all no matter what.
24. Treat others the way you want to be treated.
25. To never give up on yourself.
26. To be a strong woman.

27. How to make a decision.
28. To be loving.
29. How to keep a clean house.
30. The value of honesty.
31. Think of others before yourself.
32. That she is always there for me, and we're all crazy.
33. Everyone should be treated with kindness and respect regardless of race, gender, and economic status.
34. That family is family and you drop everything for them.
35. Love unconditionally.
36. Manners and how to clean.
37. Stay out of trouble.
38. That anyone can walk out of your life at any time, including your mother.
39. How to save money.
40. Compassion.
41. To always be myself and never let people walk over me.
42. Love Christ.
43. How to let things be as they are.
44. How to be a mother.
45. No matter how hard things get, you can make it through with the glory of God.
46. That God is in control and that ALL things or situations change.
47. Not taught, but I learned to be opposite of the way she was!
48. Work for what you want, never depend on anyone. Always work hard and be honest. And you can do anything you set your mind to.
49. Somebody is always worse off no matter what.
50. Although I love my mom dearly, she just wasn't that type of mom to teach me anything.
51. How not to raise children.
52. Don't depend on others; do it yourself.
53. That she will love me no matter what.
54. Enjoy life.
55. Never give up!

56. Respect.
57. Compassion, unconditional love, and common courtesy.
58. Never let anyone let you feel unloved, and never think you are not capable of doing anything.
59. Woman can.
60. Pursue my dreams.
61. How to push through the hardest times alone with a smile on my face.
62. It would be a tie. She taught me that there is most definitely is a God. For that, I'm eternally grateful. The other thing would be that she taught me to always look for the child in someone you don't like or agree with. If you can envision that person as they might have been as a child, there is no way you can feel hate for them. Very powerful.
63. How to duck.
64. To love others as Christ loved us.
65. That Jesus Christ is our Savior and that we can have eternal life through our faith in His death and resurrection if we repent and we believe.
66. Staying grounded in God when life throws a curve ball. Treat others with compassion like God has.
67. Faithfulness.
68. My faith.
69. How important siblings are.
70. Looking back, I think I learned that, as a mother, if you aren't taking care of yourself, you can't take care of your family. Whether it's your health, mental health, or just your sanity.
71. To love and trust God in all matters of life. She always said if you can't say something good about someone, keep your mouth shut.
72. How to handle and deal with drama. I never let drama get to me or affect me in a negative way.
73. To not take crap off anybody, take up for myself and respect.
74. Always respect the elderly, and saying no is not always a bad thing.

75. Love the Lord Jesus Christ and your family. Work or study hard and behave yourself. Visit and help the elderly; be kind to others.

76. The one thing she taught me was before you leave the house, your hair should be done, your makeup on, and a smile on your face because you didn't know who you would run into even if you were only going to the mailbox.

77. She taught me how to cook and take care of myself.

78. She taught us (maybe not by words, but mostly through her testimony) strength. She specifically taught me the importance of finding myself and my identity and being true to that person.

79. Independence.

80. Love, forgiveness, and take your meds.

Now it's your turn to answer.

What was the most important thing your mother taught you?

_____
_____
_____
_____
_____
_____
_____
_____
_____
_____
_____
_____
_____
_____
_____
_____
_____
_____
_____
_____
_____
_____
_____
_____
_____
_____

Chapter 2

What Do You Wish She Would
Have Taught You Sooner?

This would be so much easier if it were one sentence answers. As I stare out at the snow, just a beautiful few inches here in Pennsylvania. It is the beginning of March. Spring is coming, then summer, and there will be so much to do and things to get ready for. Redoing some of the flower beds out front and making new ones. I think I will add tulips and calla lilies, maybe daisies and definitely Gerber's to the beds. I need more color. How did I know how to plant flowers and what was what? This was all learned by looking things up, my husband's ideas and trial and ere. We will be getting the garden ready as well, always trying something different, always learning new ways to get things to grow better. And of course, John was laughing at me because last year, I started corn in the house and transplanted it in to the garden. Then to prove a point that I had a good idea, I planted the rest of the seeds outside. They all died! I couldn't keep up with the lack of rain we had. Don't tell him, I'm going to do it the same way this year too. I still have a point to prove!

The wood-cutting season is here; it's always here. John runs a wood ministry through our church. With his partial shoulder replacement, he has been taking a vacation from it. He will say I have had him on lock down, he would be correct. But when we started this ministry, he taught me how to use a chainsaw (I have one of my own); I also know how to use the splitter and how to drive a front end loader. I love it all.

I know how to cook, though I don't have too much. My hubby enjoys that more than I do. I do like to bake. One of my sisters remembers our mother making homemade bread. I don't, but that would have been cool to have her teach me.

When it comes to electronics, I will have to say I have learned the most from my kids. I tend to lose things and then panic when I can't find them. That has already happened on this project! Tried to save the work I had already finished to a thumb drive, nope! It ended up on another part of the desktop. At this present time, I still haven't figured that out. So I am saving, saving, and saving. Oh, and I have printed it out already. My college girl comes home for spring break soon; she can help! Sorry about the rabbit trails. How foolish of me to think I can ask others these questions for this book and not have to have my own responses figured out. I have some notes but mostly memories.

Back on trail.

I used to think learning to put makeup on was the most important thing I missed out on, along with other girl stuff. But make up was the big deal when I was thirteen. One of my first foster mothers as a teen (I had a few others from when I was tiny to fifteen) had makeup she wasn't using, so she gave it to me. I had a little bit of an idea what to do. Minus the fact the colors were all wrong, the blush looked like I was always flushed. The real laugh (not at the time) was the mascara. I would close my eyes to apply it, on the top of my lashes, and try and put it under the bottoms. For the life of me, I could not figure out how to keep it from getting all over my eyes, until I was taught on career day. Not by asking of course, but watching. I was too afraid to ask for help. I remember being so aware of every move the lady made. Not wanting to miss anything, so the next day, I would have it on right. I was too afraid to ask for help. I didn't want any of the other girls knowing I was not taught by my mother. I'm sure they figured it out.

Are we so critical of ourselves at that age that we begin to be critical of others at the same time? Is that when we are taught the older we get; the more negative and judgmental we are to be toward other females? That we have to outdo each other with everything from hair to jobs? Strong women should build each other up and show those who feel weak they really are strong. (Borrowed from a wonderful friend and sister in Christ!),

I know not all women act that way. But I have in the past. I just never wanted to look stupid. I wanted to be needed, wanted, something to offer. Something of value, someone of value, I wanted to be valued. I wasn't taught that I deserved love, friendship, and respect from my mother. Again, how can you teach what you do not know? You can't!

Did anyone ever tell her she was more precious than the most valuable stone? Proverbs 31 talks about how we as women should strive to be. Not saying perfect, but striving, trying our hardest to be the women God created us to be. I am still a work in progress! I fall short every day, but tomorrow, I will get back up and strive again!

> A wife of noble character who can find? She is worth far more than rubies. Her husband has full confidence in her and lacks nothing of value. (Proverbs 31:10–11, NIV)

> She is clothed with strength and dignity; she can laugh at the days to come. She speaks with wisdom, and faithful instruction is on her tongue. She watches over the affairs of her household and does not eat the bread of idleness. Her children arise and call her blessed; her husband also, and he praises her: "many women do noble things, but you surpass them all." (Proverbs 31:25–29, NIV)

Wow! Can you imagine being told you are worth more than rubies? That they think and feel and *know you are important!* That *you* are *priceless!* And they *know* you have whatever situation you are up against!

What does *clothed with strength and dignity* look like, a high end suit, the most expensive car? The way you handle yourself in the grocery store when the clerk says you don't have enough money to buy all of your groceries? What does it look like?

Strength: The quality of being strong. Power to resist force. Power to resist attack.

I do not always have "it" together when something goes wrong. Losing "it" in the past meant hitting walls. There have been times when the only strength I have is to hit the floor on my knees and with fists and yell at God. Yes, I have been that angry. Most of the time, it was my own doing or me thinking I could control what others did. I have not always been strong in the sense that I made the best choice in my spiritual walk. I could get angry with God quicker than I could ask Him for help.

Dignity: The quality or state of being worthy of honor and respect. A dignified look or way of behaving.

Well, see above because I haven't been very good at that one either.

The wind outside is blowing hard as the new snow falls. Looking out as the cars are going up the road is harder to see through the squalls. Am I harder to see as each day passes if I do not know my own worth? Only to myself, God sees me every day, no matter what. But with that, others will miss out on what you have to offer if we hide ourselves away out of fear. Fear that others may not see us as who we are meant to be.

Picture it: You come home from a tough day, and your mom is there, or your mom figure, maybe your husband and maybe kids. I know it may sound silly, but bear with me, I'm trying to picture this scene too. You come in, toss your things on a chair, and say, "Today was so tough. I can't do it anymore! I just don't think I can! I'm over it. I can't get anything right!"

But your mom, who is the famous cheerleader of her children, hugs you and says, "You can do this! You have so much to offer those who you see every day. Don't give up, I love you. I believe in you!"

As your eyes well up with tears, as mine are, you believe her words. It gives you a moment to breathe and a sense of self-worth. It gives you confidence to know you matter, you are needed.

Your children whom you adore say, "Mom, you rock! You always make everything better. You are strong like superman and smart too!"

"You are cool, you have kisses and band-aides, and you're the best!" I can handle that! Again, you matter, and you are needed.

Are you still with me? Can you feel the emotions churning inside of you that you can continue because even the kids have your back?

Your husband, teammate, partner in crime with nerf guns to team against the kids, or each other, your teammate in life and parenting, takes you by the shoulders. Sits you on the couch and kneels before you.

He says, "You are amazing! You are strong and caring, without you, this house would fall apart. I would be lost without you! I think others would be, too, if you give up. Without you, I could not do this. You give so much of you to others! I am honored to call you my wife, my friend!"

Now close your eyes and picture all of that for a moment.

Do you get it? Do you see the point it has taken me so long to learn and accept? If you see it, when will you believe it?

You are worthy of love, friendship, and respect!

You are worth it!

What if one person in your life said this to you? Would you believe it? Would you feel it? Would you want it? I am telling you, *you are worth it*!

"Honor her for all that her hands have done, and let her works bring her praise at the city gate" (Proverbs 31:25–29, NLT).

That's what I wish my mother would have taught me sooner. Even more than that, deeper than that, that God sees me this way! He sees me worthy of His love! He sees me! *El Roi* (El raw-ee), "the God who sees me."

> Thereafter, Hagar used another name to refer to the LORD, who had spoken to her. She said, "You are the God who sees me." She also said, "Have I truly seen the One who sees me?" So that well was named Beer-lahai-roi (which means "well of the Living One who sees me"). (Genesis 16: 13–14a, NLT)

Responses

What do you wish your mother would have taught you sooner?

1. How to budget money.
2. I wish I would have learned sooner so the hurt could have been lessened.
3. How to keep my mouth shut at the right time; actually, she taught that. I didn't always pay attention.
4. To be more open-minded toward other cultures and religion.
5. How to cook.
6. Everything that a good mother should teach all their children: strength and not to be a victim under any circumstances.
7. How to cook ethnic Polish dishes.
8. How to make her cinnamon rolls. Don't have the recipe, wish I did, and to love myself more.
9. How to love myself and self-worth.
10. That being a parent isn't easy.
11. Healthy eating and positive reflections.
12. To trust my instincts.
13. Financial responsibility.
14. How to love her as unconditionally as she loved me. She had to die to teach it to me.
15. Nothing because at age thirteen I became an adult. That's when my dad died, and I had to help her.
16. She taught what she should have at the right times. I just didn't always listen and learn.
17. About life.
18. Can't think of anything.
19. I don't think anything; she was a very wise lady.
20. Independence and confidence.
21. How to forgive others.
22. Marriage is hard work.
23. How people should treat me.

24. To be a better judge of character.
25. Too much to mention.
26. How to get by without her.
27. People aren't always kind.
28. That life is harder than she let on.
29. The birds and the bees talk.
30. How to stand on my own and be strong.
31. How she could have been a better mother.
32. How to stand up for myself.
33. To put my future first.
34. That it's okay to ask for help.
35. Wish we would've talked; she was always yelling and finding things that should've been done.
36. To open my heart to others.
37. How to pick my battles.
38. I honestly do not know how to respond to that because my mom always tried to teach us so many valuable lessons in life. I wish I would have listened to her!
39. To be more appreciative of others.
40. When to put me first.
41. That I didn't need a man's love to survive in life.
42. Patience.
43. How to live without her.
44. About God.
45. Not to give up on love.
46. To love myself.
47. Talk and walk with God.
48. About sex.
49. Love is hard.
50. How to do taxes.
51. Salvation.
52. It's okay to love yourself.
53. Working hard pays off.
54. Some self-love, how to have self-esteem and self-worth.
55. Knowing when it's okay to give up or ask for help.
56. To be ready to lose her.

57. I wish she'd have taught me sooner that it's okay to think of myself sometimes and not always put other people first.
58. How to deal with mental illness and drug abuse.
59. How to handle a true heartbroken situation.
60. Her insight into my boyfriends.
61. To sew.
62. Show me a real relationship and values.
63. How to be grounded and not let the past make me a bitter person.
64. Housekeeping LOL.
65. Sunshine on my shoulders.
66. How to pick my husband.
67. That my children really would be more than the best thing in my life, and how hard I'd struggle with giving my daughter up. But then again, that's not really something you can teach.
68. More about my dad. He died when I was fifteen.
69. To have nice things in life, you need to have good credit.
70. To take church and God more seriously. We were taught by her example; do what you want all week long then go to church and act like you do no wrong.
71. The world is cruel and to run to Jesus for comfort. God is more real than our problems; he is the answer.
72. How hard life really is and how stressful it can be at times. Also, people don't always think and act the same way as you do.
73. I was blessed; mom lived and taught me great values.
74. About love.
75. I wish I would have learned sooner that the world isn't a totally evil and dangerous place. Not everyone can be trusted but not everyone is evil. Being afraid of the world and of bad things happening can keep us from so many good things and people. I think that's something we are learning together.
76. Boys suck, maybe she did, and I just didn't listen.

Now it's your turn to answer.

What do you wish your mother would have taught you sooner?

_____

_____

_____

_____

_____

_____

_____

_____

_____

_____

_____

_____

_____

_____

_____

_____

_____

_____

_____

_____

_____

_____

_____

_____

_____

_____

_____

Chapter 3

When You Think of Your Mom, What Makes You Smile the Most?

So before I started writing this, God gave me questions. Questions I needed to think about and things I would ask others in a survey. Some of the people I have spoken with about the questions have said they are deep and difficult. They were right. I have had to sift through memories and emotions on all of them. I find I want to answer them with one-word answers, like some of you have. That would be too easy, and healing wouldn't come any time soon. I would want this question to have tons of responses from my girls. But I have not always been that good mom. I'm sure there are times in their lives when just my voice or presence would upset them or anger them. Today, as I write this, I do not believe that to be a true statement. Do I still frustrate them or make them a tad bit angry? I'm sure I do. I pray they recall the fun things more than the negative: The fake reindeer tracks on the kitchen floor Christmas morning. The jamming out to a tennis racquet on the couch because they were being grumpy teenagers. It was right after freaky Friday came out. They changed their attitude. Of course, how can you and your friend not laugh and smile after Mom tips the couch playing the tennis racquet as a guitar?

My mother didn't do a lot of that crazy kind of stuff. But she has this laugh, it's so contagious! She would laugh until she cried; I get that from her. Her green eyes would be sea green or a Christmas green; I get that from her too! She and I can't hide when we cry. The deepness of the green gives it away every time.

I sit here and laugh a little and smile. I found something that we have in common, her and I. And I am okay with it, for once. If I think back to the "good times" or the less chaotic times, there are other things that make me smile, like chocolate chip cookies baking on a spring day after school. When you walked in that house on Canterbury Street and cookies were baking, all was right with the world, and my father was not home. She would be smiling and have her hair up, with flour on her face and a look that now I can say was peace. She could breathe. She could live. She could be a mom. That makes me smile. That's when she asked me how my day was. And in those moments, she showed she cared.

She was so creative. Her paintings were awesome. The time she took to do them, the steady hands needed. I remember when she got this pattern for the cabbage patch dolls. It's when they first came out and my parents couldn't afford to buy them. But she got her hands on these patterns and made about five or six of them. Some were babies and others had hair. She would dress them in cute clothes. They were the greatest thing I had ever seen her make! Over and over again, she would ask what we thought of them. She needed that reassurance she had done something great. I know where I get it. Then there were the holly hobby dolls she made as well. She made me one. And it was the most perfect doll in the whole world. She didn't buy the clothes for her. She made them by hand. Everything was by hand. My mother didn't own a sewing machine. The faces were perfect, the colors of the hair and eyes, the cheeks with just the right color. The dresses and bloomers were amazing. She made bloomers for my holly hobby doll! She was so proud of that doll. I was so proud of her. I was so excited to get the best doll in the world. I don't know what she spent to make it, but the time was to be appreciated and treasured. And it was. I don't have her now. The last time I got taken from them, I had to leave her behind.

But I can still picture that doll in my hands. Her hair and eyes matched mine. She had a smile. I smiled when I held her, when I hugged her, when I loved her, when I loved my mom. When I knew in my heart my mommy must have loved me enough to make this amazing holly hobby doll, just for me!

It's so hard not to cry. So I just do. I cry for the love I knew I had at one time, the best way she could show it. I cry for the love that went into the doll as if she had a chance to do it all over. I cry because watching her love and hold those creations she made, I wanted held and loved more than them. I cry because she did make me smile at times, and I miss it. I miss her when she had those moments. I smile because for a short time, I had that moment. I smile for the sea-green eyes we share, the love for making things for our children, the joy they show when we gave them the things we made.

I know how she felt, and my heart smiles. I know that, for a brief moment in time, my mom felt loved, needed, wanted, treasured. She felt like a mom. And I miss her.

I don't want to miss her until I'm angry anymore. I just want to miss her and remember and move on without the pain and without the hurt. I want to miss her without feeling mad at myself for doing so. Without feeling angry because I can't always be tough. I don't want to emotionally beat myself up for wanting what I can't have. I want to just have the ability to smile because I love her, because I miss her. And knowing she was a mom, at times, that needs remembered. I would love to be able to tell her again how much I was grateful for the time and money she spent on my doll. And hug her and my doll again. Thank you for the smiles today, Mom, in my heart and on my face.

> But God demonstrates his own love for us in this: while we were still sinners, Christ died for us. (Romans 5:8, NIV)

> You have made known to me the path of life; you will fill me with joy in your presence, with eternal pleasures at your right hand. (Psalm 16:11, NIV)

Splendor and majesty are before him; strength and joy in his dwelling place. (1 Chronicles 16:27, NIV)

The precepts of the Lord are right, giving joy to the heart. The commands of the Lord are radiant, giving light to the eyes. (Psalm 19:8, NIV)

Responses

When you think of your mom, what makes you smile most?

There were many duplicate answers to this question, so I tried to only add duplicates once.

1. Her smile.
2. That people say I look or sound like her, it's an honor.
3. Her laugh.
4. She was always helping my dad. I remember her cooking a lot.
5. When she did artwork or baked bread.
6. Fun times we had as a child.
7. Knowing she was always there for me no matter what.
8. Her love for my dad.
9. Her gentle spirit!
10. Talks we had.
11. Her naïve and congenial nature.
12. Her love and laughter.
13. Supper time, she happily served amazing meals every day at 5:00 p.m.
14. Her kindness and humor.
15. How much she loved her grandchildren.
16. Her strength and she still hangs her clothes outside at age eighty-nine!
17. The fact that she raised seven children on her own after Dad died.
18. Everything about her.
19. Her beautiful singing voice.
20. That she was there for me when I gave birth to all my kids.
21. Her concern for her family.
22. Her love.
23. Her love of nature.
24. Her determination.
25. Her advice.
26. Our relationship.

27. The way she can laugh so hard at things that she cries. When we are together and this happens, it is truly hysterical.
28. Her sense of humor.
29. *She was always there for me.*
30. She tried her best.
31. Her smile and joy children.
32. How her children always came first.
33. She sings old songs; her cooking is amazing.
34. Her love for me and others.
35. Her cooking.
36. Her wisdom and all the great family times we had while she was alive.
37. She always found a way.
38. Money was always tight, but she always got me and my sisters brand-new winter coats each winter. And brand-new swimsuits in the summer.
39. She was always there for me.
40. The fact that I love her and miss her.
41. Playing cards.
42. She's the most selfless person I know.
43. Her attitude, she was a smart butt.
44. Remembering going to yard sales, and when she would find something she wanted, how excited she would get!
45. Her mixing up all our names when she calls for us.
46. Halloween.
47. Everything now.
48. The stories my mom tells and the jokes we share.
49. Moving out.
50. Her stability.
51. Her fierce love for her grandchildren.
52. She is a caring person.
53. There were seven *nothing* responses.
54. The love she had for her two biological children and her ten adopted special-needs children.
55. Too many things to write about, but her love and sense of humor are the top two.

56. Her *beautiful* singing voice!
57. Her singing, as a child when she wasn't working three jobs and stressing and taking care of everyone but herself. I can still smell her perfume, and she would clean the house listening to the radio and hearing her sing made me happy.
58. The measures she took to ensure the well-being and safety of her children.
59. She gave the best hugs.
60. Taking me to Memaw's house.
61. The short period of time she took antidepressants.
62. Mighty spirit.
63. How much she gave up for me and my sisters because she was doing it as a single mom.
64. She loved unconditionally.
65. What a good woman of God she was.
66. Her silliness.
67. Her zest for life.
68. The memories we share.
69. Her jokes.
70. Her generosity and unconditional love.
71. The way she loves my children.
72. Her brilliance.
73. How close we are.
74. Our friendship.
75. Her smile, for years she hardly ever smiled. So to see her smile now is everything.
76. As a single mother raising two sons, she always made sure we did not go without.
77. Thinking of doing things for my mom such as cleaning and helping fix things around the house. When she is happy, it makes me smile.
78. Going to relatives, playing board games, and putting puzzles together.
79. Her always telling us it was later than it was, so we would always be early or on time for everything and her sweet voice.

80. Mom loved me unconditionally. She would bake and buy goodies for us.
81. In the present time, we can spend time together knowing now she loves me. When I was small, it was different. I never smile. I don't even know if she loved me. It wasn't until my fiftieth that she told me she loved me and it was true.
82. Our road trips.
83. She is a mom to everyone. All of my friends and my sibling's friends became her kids too. And she loves and protects them as she would her own. She is also very supportive of me. She loves me and doesn't want me to move out or move away, but she refuses to sway me from any calling God places on my life—no matter how difficult it may be to experience physical distance from each other.
84. Her brutal honesty.
85. How selfless she is.

Now it's your turn to answer.

When you think of your mom, what makes you smile the most?

_____
_____
_____
_____
_____
_____
_____
_____
_____
_____
_____
_____
_____
_____
_____
_____
_____
_____
_____
_____
_____
_____
_____
_____
_____
_____
_____
_____
_____

Chapter 4

If Your Mother Was a Song, What Would It Be?

With all the different choices of music out there, it should be hard to choose just one. But it's not. Here I go again—W.

Why? Have you heard that one?

Never knowing where I am going because of their choices. Knowing where I have been was not the best, always wasting time hoping to have a mother that was there in the currents of my life. Wanting to know why it can't be better on her part and asking God to guide me on the lonely streets of dreams. Knowing He is the only one who could help. She was just not there when it counted. Feeling destined to be alone. Alone, abandoned, unwanted, and searching, always returning to repeat the last road walked and always leaving our home because she could not care for me and because of my father too.

I'm sure I could come up with others that would describe how being her child felt most of the time. This is one that is the nicest that says most of how I feel. She lived the same, so she was gone often, not there emotionally. Maybe she felt like I did, always looking for answers and needing charity to fix her broken heart and dreams. Maybe she always worried about what was next, never having answers.

"Therefore, do not worry about tomorrow, for tomorrow will worry about itself. Each day has enough trouble of its own" (Matthew 6:34, NIV).

In my Bible, that scripture is in red. That is Jesus talking. Giving me, us, direct instruction on how to handle the future issues of tomorrow. If I keep that above song as my song of childhood or adulthood, I am worrying about tomorrow way too much! There are enough problems in tomorrow that if I focus on it, I am missing today. If I am missing today, I may very well miss what God has in line for me, the blessings and the ability to walk with others. I'm not saying now that song was wrong for me. It's as real as a five-hundred-pound bull in a pen, standing there facing me, ready to charge. I just don't want to live it anymore. I don't want my mother to live it anymore either.

So how about a few that say who I am and the songs I wish would say who my mom really is. I know how God sees her, but I want to see her the way he does to.

"God, Help Me"—Plumb

"Fight Song"—Rachel Platten

"I Am Beautiful"—Candice Glover

"Lord, I'm Ready Now"—Plumb

"Redeemed"—Big Daddy Weave

"Come as You Are"—Crowder

"Beautiful"—Mercy Me

"Clean"—Natalie Grant

"I Surrender All"

What is your new song for yourself or your mother figure? If it was good, don't change it. If you are still a little to broken to change it, it will come. I am praying for all who need the heavy chains broken. You can be redeemed! You can have freedom from the pain. Join me, in not being who we used to be, thank God, redeemed!

> But I will sing of your strength, in the morning I will sing of your love; for you are my fortress, my refuge in times of trouble. You are my strength, I sing praise to you; you God are my fortress, my God on whom I can rely. (Psalm 59:16–17)

> Satisfy us in the morning with your unfailing love, so that we may sing for joy and be glad all our days. (Psalm 90:14, NIV)

Responses

If she was a song, what would it be?

(The numbers at the end are how many responses that picked that song.)

1. We Can Work It Out
2. Fight Song
3. Mama's Broken Heart
4. Female
5. Crazy B
6. Heavenly Sunshine
7. Wind Beneath My Wings (8)
8. Thank God and the Greyhound She's Gone
9. I'd Rather Have Jesus
10. One Day at a Time Sweet Jesus
11. His Eye Is on the Sparrow
12. I'll Always Be There
13. Snow Bird
14. Love for Everyone
15. A Folk Song
16. The Twist
17. Love Me Tender
18. You Are My Sunshine (5)
19. A Mother's Love
20. Hallelujah
21. I Love This Bar
22. Celebration
23. I've Been Touched
24. I Hope You Dance
25. The Best Day (2)
26. Forever and Ever Amen
27. Broken Road
28. Bad to the Bone
29. The Hand That Rocks the Cradle
30. Rap Music

31. Because of You
32. Bad Blood (2)
33. Let It Be
34. Earth Angel
35. Over You
36. The Rose
37. Jesus Loves Me
38. Anyways
39. You Are So Beautiful
40. Turn Your Eyes upon Jesus
41. I Will Survive
42. A Coal Miner's Daughter
43. Sweet Child of Mine
44. Hurt
45. It Is Well
46. Pencil Case (kids show song)
47. F You
48. Your Name Is Glorious
49. My Girl
50. How Great Thou Art
51. In the Garden
52. Hero
53. Mighty Mouse Theme Song
54. Wings of a Dove
55. Sunshine on my Shoulders (2)
56. Oh How I Love Jesus
57. In My Daughter's Eyes (2)
58. Angel
59. Close to You (2)
60. Some People Change
61. Amazing Grace (2)
62. Daisy Day
63. No Place That Far
64. Mama's Song
65. Like My Mother Does

Now it's your turn to answer.

If she was a song, what would it be?

_____
_____
_____
_____
_____
_____
_____
_____
_____
_____
_____
_____
_____
_____
_____
_____
_____
_____
_____
_____
_____
_____
_____
_____
_____
_____
_____

Chapter 5

If She Were a Flower

When I think of flowers, I think of beauty, the vibrant colors, exotic smells, simple smells with promise of something to come. Like the dozen roses on my counter now. My husband handed them to me saying Merry Christmas and just because. Just because why? Maybe it's "I have space on the island or counter that they can go." Or I have the vases that need used. Maybe the house needs brightened up by the mere presence and smell of fresh roses. So as preparing for this chapter and reading the responses others sent to me, I found it difficult to come up with a flower to describe my mother. Maybe I should pick a rose because it matches her name; or carnations because they grew in the yard, and there were a lot of them, many different colors, and she loved them. How about the opposite direction, and say marigolds because I don't like the smell? Not that she smelled bad, I just don't like them. They make me sneeze and are just annoying but very useful for keeping pests out of a garden but not useful to me. Maybe she was the pest in my life. So if I want to be mean, I supposed a marigold would fit. But there was a beauty to my mother that few got to see. They didn't see her bloom in happiness. Now that I think of it, I hardly saw any of that.

When I think of blooming flowers, I think of newborn babies. It is possibly because when our youngest daughter was born, I woke up to a dozen roses at my bedside. When they start to open up and bloom, I feel like it is new life showing itself. I wonder what my mother thought when I was born. Was I wonderful? Did she smile? Did she want to hold me close? I don't know. She never talked about that. The only thing I ever heard was my father showed up drunk to the hospital, and the police had to remove him. He was causing problems as always. That is all she or anyone ever said about my birth. I don't know how big or little I was or if I was healthy. If the drugs she took and the alcohol she drank affected me. How do I know this? I was in and out of foster care as a small child until fifteen. I have seen the files at CYS in Eugene, Oregon. So I know all of the reasons I was removed and what was or not done to get me back each time. From twelve on, she quit trying. I never went back to live with them again.

With that information, I want to pick a flower I like. But the flower is to be as if it were her. I wish it were a rhododendron, a flowering plant that has the potential to be huge and mighty with branches and flowers to help shield you from the wind. Or the different kinds of lilies with vibrant colors that grow in even the not-so-great soil. Hearty stems with multiple bulbs pushing through, giving year after year to bring joy and a sense of peace when they are admired. But neither of those fit.

I think a pansy. I grow them in my flower beds, and they are beautiful. Have you ever looked at the detail in them? Some of the colors are so fascinating to me. The multicolored are my favorite. They can tolerate some changes in weather like a hard spring rain yet still very delicate when you plant them. They are easily damaged if you're not gentle enough. And sometimes, I am in a rush to plant so I mess some up. So my mother is a beautifully complicated flower, depending on how she is treated. But when she had strength, back my mother in a corner, and you may see a tiger lily appear.

> The grass withers and the flowers fall, but the word of God endures forever. (Isaiah 40:8, NIV)

> Do everything in love. (1 Corinthians 16:14, NIV)

Your beauty should not come from outward adornment, such as elaborate hairstyles and the wearing of gold jewelry or fine clothes. Rather, it should be that of your inner self, the unfading beauty of a gentle and quiet spirit, which is of great worth in God's sight. (1 Peter 3:3–4, NIV)

Responses

If she were a flower?

1. Tulip (8)
2. Black rose (2)
3. Fox glove (2)
4. Lilac (5)
5. Rose (for beauty) (14)
6. Rose with thorns (8)
7. Pansies
8. Yellow rose (7)
9. Daffodil (2)
10. Peonies (3)
11. Daisy (10)
12. Ivy flowers
13. Lily (12)
14. Dandelion (6)
15. Sunflower (3)
16. Rose (it has many layers)
17. Iris
18. Bird of paradise
19. Carnation
20. Petunias
21. Thistle
22. Magnolia
23. Weeds
24. Poppy
25. Yellow apricot flower
26. Thorns
27. Morning glory
28. Gardenia
29. Hyacinth
30. Venus fly trap
31. Brown-eyed Susan (2)
32. Blooming Orchid

33. Aloe flower
34. Bleeding heart
35. Marigold
36. Violet
37. Wild flower

Now it's your turn to answer.

If she were a flower?

_____
_____
_____
_____
_____
_____
_____
_____
_____
_____
_____
_____
_____
_____
_____
_____
_____
_____
_____
_____
_____
_____
_____
_____
_____
_____
_____
_____

Chapter 6

If Your Mother Was a Book

I t's snowing today in Pennsylvania. again. Absolutely breathtaking. I love how it sits on the branches of the trees as if it's afraid to fall. It's so very cold though, only nineteen degrees out. I was thinking about curling up in the living room, in the big, round, soft chair by one of the two Christmas trees with a good book. Not today, or at least not right now. This one is more important to write. And that happens to be the question we are on. If my mother was a book, what would she be? On my copy of the questionnaire, it is blank. As were many of the ones that some of you did.

So far, I have 108 questionnaires returned, with a deadline of thirty-two days. Out of those 108, 46 had no answer. So you can see it's not an easy question. I remember looking at these questions after I typed them out on my phone thinking this is insane. I told my pastor I typed them out during someone preaching the message on a Sunday morning. I just could not get my mind off the book idea from the afternoon before! I found as I sat there, lost in my thoughts of other moms and their adult children relationships, nothing else could get through. I had watched one of my friends the day before with her mom, working together to set up a birthday party for her kids. I knew the relationship wasn't always great, but for that time, they were a team! It was so cool to watch. I wanted that!

I wanted to know how the other women there were with their moms. So I started asking. They were different responses, and that made me think even more of how I wanted to know if my mother and I could work together on something like this. That's when the idea came for this. One of my friends said write about it. Well, as you can tell, that's all I could think about.

I know that God laid these questions on my heart. They came so quickly. But the answer's not so quick. He is making me think and dig and feel. And feel. And feel.

I have read a lot of different books. And out of all of them, I could pick little pieces and sentences or paragraphs. Maybe, even whole chapters but not just one book. With the answers I have received already, man there are some interesting ones. None that fit my mom though!

So I will create my own. The title: Layers of her.

We can take a part from a child's book, Are You My Mother. Over and over again, asking that question, are you my mother? I don't need to ask that, I know. But then I wonder if you didn't want me, why didn't you just give me to someone who would want me and love me? It's like getting your two-year-old a puppy for Christmas, why would you make that choice? Was I just there for you to say, "Oh look, I have yet another kid to take care of?" Are you my mother? Not really. Not in behavior. Not in a loving manner. Maybe the title should be why don't you want to be my mother? At least, the title would imply the truth that you didn't want to be my mother.

Love you to the moon and back, just one page. I think I chose this title because it's what I want you to say to me. Yes, even now as an adult. I want to know that there is nothing that separates the love you could have for me, not pain, distance, nothing. And the space in between the moon and me is full of your love.

Where the wild things are for the bad moods you always seemed to have. I understand your moods; I wish mine were understood sometimes. The difference between you and I, I am learning how not to direct them at the kids or the innocent ones. I still fail on it but have also learned how to apologize and ask for forgiveness for it and try not to do it again. It has taken many years, and I still make the wrong choice, but I never quit trying to do better. I think I know I am mad at you for never telling me you were sorry, for anything you caused that I didn't earn.

Secret garden, though there are beautiful things in a garden, there is also pain. Pain so deep it makes the owner close off what used to bring joy. He also closed his heart to those around him, and he ignored what others needed from him. So no matter how beautiful you were, my heart was closed to anyone that had a mom title. You would all be the same, no matter what I did or what any of you tried. I didn't need another trying to grow in my heart just to be taken over by weeds and left all alone in a closed-up space.

And I realized now, years later, I owe someone an apology. She left me too, but she tried to love me. She tried to be what you couldn't. I cut that flower down before it could grow to be a wonderful bloom of vibrant color and love. So I say M.M., I am sorry for hurting you. You didn't have the information booklet on how to help this flower grow. And I wasn't about to let you learn. I pray you realize this paragraph is about you. I pray for forgiveness someday. Yes, I know the wounds and words cut deep. The actions were just as bad. I am sorry, please forgive me.

Go dog go for some silliness. You could laugh like no other. The silliness and fun we had sometimes, I miss. I don't want to miss it, it hurts. So I laugh. I find the silliness like you to hide the pain. And I am just as silly as you sometimes, in a good way LOL. Remember the times you would brush you thick red hair with your head leaning forward? And then flip your hair back, you had a lion's mane! Ha-ha I can't help but laugh. Sometimes, I do that. Just to remember you in a good memory. I miss your laugh. I miss your smile. I miss you.

Darn, this is hard! Why does God call me and others to heal this way?

Nope, didn't get an answer.

Yes, that is my way of stopping the pain and tears for a moment. Why is it important to express when tears come or anger or pain? Because the walls have to come down, and I have to share that it really can happen to show that the heart is not as black as coal or as cold as ice. That as hard as I want to be, I'm not always.

And the rest will be about a woman who had no strength to fight. She suffered with drug use and depression, possibly other mental health issues. (I'm not putting her down for mental health problems.) No knowledge on how to survive other than going away or shutting down. A horror story where she is stuck in life-threatening moments with fear and pain with a slim chance of survival. She will run up stairs and back into a house instead of a police car waiting out front. It will take a while to get out of the house because she just doesn't know how to turn the doorknob.

She will battle death internally. How can a heart live with all of this pain? Being alone and far away from those who could have helped, but yet, she denied their existence too often. And it can end with a miracle, of God saving her when she was almost out of breath! He will move her to a safe place. He will put police officers in her life that help save her. She will see the doorknob, and she will instantly know how to use it. She will get out! She does get out!

She will still have struggles, but she will know the name of Jesus. She will know salvation and redemption. She will have moments she forgets that she has been redeemed.

She will still hide the fear and bad choices she made before. Fear of being rejected will always linger. Relationships will at least have a chance for some sort of healing. Maybe not the way she needs or wants fully, but at least, some holes will be filled in again with truth and forgiveness. And now she can breathe; she can inhale and exhale without fear of not knowing how it could have been. Even if just a little peace comes, it is still peace, and it will still come. And Jesus will still be her Savior, and he will always love her for who she is for her many layers.

> Let the peace of Christ rule in your hearts, since as members of one body you were called to peace. And be thankful. Let the word of Christ dwell in you richly as you teach and admonish one another with all wisdom, and as you sing psalms, hymns and spiritual songs with gratitude in your hearts to God. And whatever you do, whether in word or deed, do it all in the name of the Lord Jesus, giving thanks to God the Father through him. (Colossians 3:15–17, NIV)

Responses

If she were a book? There were not a lot of responses for this one.

1. How to treat a stepchild like crap.
2. I think a children's book full of wonderful stories.
3. A song book, she had a song for every occasion.
4. Song of fire and ice.
5. Ruth – in the Bible. (2)
6. Inspirational.
7. It would be religious.
8. A mystery.
9. How to get a man and get rid of them.
10. The encyclopedia.
11. Little woman.
12. A Bible. (6)
13. Mother Goose.
14. Hmm not sure, one in which there are a lot of struggle but also triumphs.
15. Magazines.
16. The giving tree.
17. Do it yourself.
18. Dr. S. because her words stay with you the way you remember a simple verse. Although it may be simple, the meaning is great.
19. A biography.
20. A JC Book: ups and downs and a lot of humor to keep you going.
21. Not everything was perfect but love found a way.
22. Love and laughter.
23. Moby Dick (she would be the whale).
24. Little House on the Prairie.
25. Romance
26. Old Testament.

27. The emotional-absent mother: A guide to self-healing and getting the love you missed.
28. Soup recipe book.
29. Love you forever.
30. 13 Reasons Why.
31. Nonfiction.
32. Dante's Inferno.
33. Something along the lines of an E.B. book.
34. Ode to the distant one, unless you are someone to impress.
35. Through her eyes, a mother's love.
36. Present over perfect.
37. Mother Goose.
38. Flowers in the attic.
39. It.
40. The Secret Garden.
41. Are You There, God? It's me Margaret.
42. Love you forever.
43. Oh, the places you'll go.
44. The Guernsey literary and potato peel pie society.
45. Dusty red book that's super thick.
46. Lies women believe (I think she really hates herself for her mistakes, her body, and her depression).
47. A docudrama.
48. Twilight Zone.
49. When helping hurts.
50. Anne of Green Gables.
51. Green eggs and ham.
52. Hard cover.
53. She said yes: my mom has never backed down from what she believes in.
54. She would be portraying the school of hard knocks.
55. The life God blesses.
56. One that is fiction because she was always fake in public or around people. She was very different than at home.
57. She would be a survival guide on how to survive the wilderness with being bipolar.

Now it's your turn to answer.

If she were a book?

_____

_____

_____

_____

_____

_____

_____

_____

_____

_____

_____

_____

_____

_____

_____

_____

_____

_____

_____

_____

_____

_____

_____

_____

_____

_____

Chapter 7

What Smell Reminds You of Her?

Of all the senses I have, this is the one I actually struggle with the most. Touch is second. But smell, man, that is totally first in the trouble department. Everything around us has a smell. It doesn't matter if it is pleasant, horrible, disgusting, sweet, fresh, or old. It's always something.

There are multiple smells that remind me of my mother. One is no higher on the scale of memory than the others. They are just smells that trigger memories, pain or positive.

I have to say this question shut me down for a few days. I didn't write anything. I just spent time looking over and absorbing your answers. No, I wasn't trying to cheat and borrow answers from some of you. LOL. Although, do you realize how much easier that would be right now? And then I ask God, why this question? Why do I need to care? Is it so when I smell a certain odor, it doesn't send me back to a place I don't want to visit again? Is figuring out what smell reminds me of her supposed to help me heal from pain that she caused or didn't stop? Well? I'm waiting . . .

I wonder how many of you are waiting for that answer too. I have heard people say they don't remember what their loved one smelled like anymore. Or their scent was off an article of clothing or a pillow they kept. But who says I want to remember her smell or a smell that puts her face in my mind? Yes, I think I am arguing with God on this one. It's not the first disagreement during this book project! By the way, the score is God–all wins, Christy–all loses. The positive is I know in my heart and mind that the final score for me, and hopefully you, will be us—healing!

I love rabbit trails, keeps me from answering right away! Ha-ha-ha!

Okay, back to reality of smells. Wait, one more question, how many of you can walk into a Yankee candle store for more than five minutes at a time? Not me! LOL, it's too over powering yet beautiful at the same time. Chocolate chip cookies! Love them, love the taste, the smell, the chocolate, the choice to make them crunchy for milk or soft. I make them; she made them. But I don't think of her every time I make them. It's a positive scent, so why wouldn't I picture her at any point?

For me, I think it is the negative smells that make me remember things quicker. Bad odors trigger my senses and memory much faster. Some the of the smells that remind me of my mother is cigarette smoke, weed, green beans and tater tot meatloaf, paint.

I hated that smell of cigs but ended up smoking myself. Hated the smell of weed, did it myself. Weed meant she was going to laugh *a lot*! She was calm and funny. Still hated the smell of green beans, ugh I still refuse to eat them. I won't cook them either. She used to make this gross meatloaf, and on top of it was a layer of tater tots and then green beans. Next to liver, that was the most disgusting dish I have ever smelled in my life! But you tell her it's good, get seconds because there wasn't always meat in the house. And sometimes, groceries were scarce. With seven people to feed, two or three dogs, a cat, and for a while a ferret and a snake, groceries and money limited but not drugs. That wasn't all her doing though.

When we smelled paint, it meant leave her alone. I tried watching her a few times but talked too much. Or I would try and show her things. I can't paint and look at your stuff at the same time; it meant leave her alone. Let her get lost in her own thoughts or the picture she was painting. I did love what she painted. It was the big velvet paintings she would do that we had to give her space for. They were probably four-feet wide, and she would hang them on the wall to paint them. Sometimes, the detail was so impressive she needed a needle to paint parts of it. The one I remember the most was of a waterfall and an angel walking two small children across a bridge. Whenever I see that picture, I think of her. When she did the tri-chem, we could be with her. We got to spend quality time with her then. Worm bookmarks and a bookmark with a book on it, we got to do those. Hours of painting with her and asking questions just to hear her voice in a loving tone. I liked getting encouragement from her that I was doing a good job.

The cold smell of snow reminds me of her. Maybe, just maybe, the smells of chocolate chips cookies and the snow are to allow my face to smile. And if my face smiles, then my heart must smile for positive memories of a woman I have fought hard to be angry at. Fought to forget, I think almost impossible. I think God is trying to show me I can have good memories, and then my heart does not stay cold and hard toward her. Then I do not stay bitter because bitterness wounds the heart like an arrow into a target, puncturing it beyond repair. Unless you allow God in, let him work in you, let him love you. Then you can learn to love back.

> A happy heart makes the face cheerful, but heart-ache crushes the spirit. (Proverbs 15:13, NIV)

> But thanks be to God, who always leads us as captives in Christ's triumphal procession and uses us to spread the aroma of the knowledge of him everywhere. (2 Corinthians 2:14, NIV)

Responses

What smell reminds you of her?

1. Perfume. (19)
2. A fresh smell, like sheets on the line.
3. Fried chicken.
4. Roses, flowers, mint tea, cinnamon, and spicy food.
5. Lilacs. (3)
6. Vanilla candles.
7. Homemade bread. (3)
8. Christmas apple.
9. Sauce and meatballs or hair care products.
10. Vodka.
11. Spaghetti, she cooked it often.
12. Fresh laundry.
13. Her cooking. (4)
14. A date nut cookie, Noxzema cream, Italian chicken (her recipe), Tabu cologne. I still have part of a bottle in my medicine cabinet, and she passed away 2/6/1992.
15. Clean laundry.
16. A fresh rain.
17. Moth balls, seriously she stored everything in moth balls. (2)
18. Milk pie.
19. Bleach.
20. Flowers and old lady perfume.
21. The smell of city chicken cooking.
22. Lavender
23. Oil of Olay. (3)
24. Fried potatoes and Charlie perfume.
25. Hair dye.
26. Pumpkin rolls, ham pot pie, and pork and sauerkraut.
27. Fresh-baked cookies.
28. Clean soap.
29. Burnt food. (2)
30. Cleaning supplies. (2)

31. Turkey.
32. Hospital, always working.
33. Pork chops and gravy.
34. Baked goods.
35. Lily of the valley.
36. Beans.
37. Honest sweat. (2)
38. Coffee. (2)
39. Pumpkin pie.
40. Lasagna baking.
41. Tide detergent.
42. Linen and soap.
43. Her smell. She has a comforting, clean scent that I can still pick out. When I was eight and she went to basic training, I stole her pillow to sleep with because it smelled like her. I still have that pillow.
44. Sunflowers.
45. Chocolate chip cookies.
46. Autumn.
47. Downy fabric softener and shower-to-shower baby powder.
48. Meatloaf.
49. Fresh open air.
50. Baby powder. (2)
51. Baking apples.
52. Roses. (2)
53. Vanilla.
54. Violet.
55. Apple pie.
56. Downy dryer sheets and an ashtray.
57. Fire burning.
58. Cigarettes, she smoked all her life. She started at a young age.
59. Roses and chocolate chip cookies.
60. Vanilla bean.
61. Her chest at the end of her bed—full of t-shirts.
62. Her house.

Now it's your turn to answer.

What smell reminds you of her?

_____
_____
_____
_____
_____
_____
_____
_____
_____
_____
_____
_____
_____
_____
_____
_____
_____
_____
_____
_____
_____
_____
_____
_____
_____
_____

Chapter 8

When You Were Sick, How Did She Take Care of You?

I know when my kids get sick, I feel helpless to a degree. Even at my worst moments as a mom, through the ignorance or choices I made, my sick kids came first. They needed me most then. Sometimes, I second-guessed myself whether I was doing enough for them. Wondering if I was waiting too long to take them to the doctors. If I was over reacting, that one got a first thought, not a second. I refused to let them suffer. I'm not hinting that my mother let me suffer. I just believe that with limited finances and moments of not emotionally being there, things were put off as long as they could be.

Even now, if the kids get sick, I hate it. A few of the kids are a couple of hours away. And that means a handful of grandchildren are a few hours away. I try not to bother them then but find myself texting often to see how they are doing. It could be one of the daughter's sick or a little one with a high fever. I worry just the same.

My college girl gets sick, and my first thought is should I go help her. I know, let her grow up. But I'm *Mom*!

Mom is supposed to kiss the booboos, put on band-aides, hold their hair when they are throwing up, get the cool wash cloth, wash the bedding if needed. All these things I don't do anymore since they are older. Unless they happen to be home, then I get to take care of them. Sometimes, Grammy and Poppy get to take care of sick little ones. It breaks my heart when these little balls of energy are curled up watching cartoons and not wanting to run and scream, or harass the dog.

So now I get to go way back to when I would get sick. I hated staying home sick! It was worse if she left me with my father. If I was vomiting or running a high fever, he left me alone. Now that I think about it, I never saw him when I was that sick. I had two older sisters that made sure I had what I needed if our mother wasn't there or busy.

There were times that she really went out of her way to take care of me, like when all five of us kids got the chicken pox. I always had everything last. So by the time I got whatever it was, everyone else was over it. My mother made sure I was covered with calamine lotion to keep from scratching the spots open. She put a cool wash cloth on my forehead when the fever got high. I got chicken broth made from the bouillon cubes to sip, chicken noodle soup, dark toast with a tiny bit of butter or crackers, and my very own 7up or ginger ale.

She always told me to rest, and she was there if I needed her, just yell for her. Just yell for her. I find myself thinking ahead, forgetting that it is about when I was sick. Wanting to lash out for other reasons because of the "just yell for her."

It was only meant for when I was sick, lying in bed or in the bathroom sick never any other time. I don't know if anyone else in my family felt that way, but I did. Of course, the need to make excuses for her arises. She needed a break. She had five kids to care for daily. Her husband was a real piece of work, not in a good way either. Maybe hearing "Mom" all day, all afternoon, and evenings was too much. Would I even want to know if it were because she was just selfish and didn't want to be a mother?

A few years ago, one of my sisters and I went down south because our mother had a stroke. We had no idea how bad or what we were walking in to. My point is, I got on a plane, flew all day, got a rental, got my sister, got lost looking for the nursing home (thank you officer who said, "let me lead you"), got us to where she was. We didn't hesitate to go. My sister said she had to, and she needed me to go with her. We went. I went for my sister. I went so she wasn't alone. I don't know that I even liked my mother enough to go, but I did.

Even though I didn't want to give her the chance to say, "You came because I needed you," I went.

And "just yell for her" was only when I was sick?

I must apologize because sometimes my heart hurts, and I get angry. I get angry because it's easier than letting my heart hurt. It is a vicious cycle that just repeats its self, until I give it to God to mend. I really just want to stop writing sometimes. I feel like my heart gets wounded and then starts to heal and then an infection comes along and undoes the healing. Maybe that's what it takes sometimes. It's almost like each layer has to get better first, but the outside hurries up and scabs. So the work has to start again and again. That is why I believe there are so many questions to this work. Each question is a new layer that needs medicated and air, love, and gentleness to heal properly.

How many layers do you have? How many more do you need to work through for healing to truly come?

In my notes, there are other memories that my mother was there for me when I was sick or injured. When I was a few years old, someone was swinging me by my arms face down. They said close your mouth. I did but ended up biting my tongue so bad, my tooth went through the section below my lower lips. I remember blood everywhere. Someone called my mother and grandmother, and they rushed me with a towel on my mouth to the hospital. I remember the look on her face was scared. There was a lot of blood; I was scared and crying. But she was there, holding me, loving me, being a great mother.

I said it; I said she was being a great mother. She really was though. I remember it so clearly. I only wish she had continued to be that great mother.

> If my people, who are called by my name, will humble themselves and pray and seek my face and turn from their wicked ways, then I will hear from heaven, and I will forgive their sin and will heal their land. (2 Chronicles 7:14, NIV)

Have mercy on me, Lord, for I am faint; heal me, Lord, for my bones are in agony. (Psalm 6:2, NIV)

The Lord sustains them on their sickbed and restores them from their bed of illness. (Psalm 41:3, NIV)

The Lord nurses them when they are sick and restores them to health. (Psalm 41:3, NLT)

"O LORD," I prayed, "have mercy on me. Heal me, for I have sinned against you." (Psalm 41:4, NLT)

I said, "Have mercy on me, LORD; heal me, for I have sinned against you." (Psalm 41:4, NIV)

He heals the brokenhearted and binds up their wounds. (Psalm 147:3, NIV)

Responses

When you were sick, how did she take care of you?

1. Very well, very nurturing.
2. Took me to the doctor. (5)
3. Oh, she is a nurse, so I got the best care there is. Cool bath for a fever, lots of liquids for a cold, a paste made from baking soda for a bee sting, and painted pink with calamine lotion when I had the chicken pox and measles. And lots of prayer.
4. She would read to me.
5. One time when I was little, I was really sick; mother called my aunt over, and they took me to the hospital. I ended up needing a spinal tap. She took good care of me when I was sick.
6. Not very well, unfortunately. (2)
7. Bring me medicine and soup. Give me a bucket to puke in.
8. Gave me medicine and sent me to bed.
9. She would make sure I had plenty of rest and took lots of vitamin C!
10. Babied me.
11. Brought me tea and toast. When she had to work, she would call home to check on me.
12. She was always there, took care of me. She would buy me coloring books and paper dolls. She would keep me covered and warm. Made sure I took my meds and followed the doctor's orders. She would also run her fingers through my hair or rub my feet.
13. She was wonderful. She served soup and toast while I watched TV on the couch.
14. Hold me on her lap.
15. Like a mother should.
16. Held me in her arms and gave me whatever I needed.
17. Brought me meals in bed.
18. She didn't, I took care of myself. (2)

19. She would never leave our side.
20. Chicken noodle soup and a kiss.
21. She would heat me up soup and check on me.
22. Chicken soup, grilled cheese, and a frozen coke.
23. She would make sure I got rest.
24. She would let me stay on the couch and she would cover me up and cook me soup. She would let me watch TV and just love me.
25. Best she could, she worked.
26. Vicks vapor rub and love.
27. Lots of soup, gave us our medicine, and bundled in a blanket.
28. Played games with me to pass the time.
29. With love, but being from a large family, she couldn't dote.
30. Always made me hot toddy and chocolate pudding, my fav.
31. Excellent care, soup, Jell-O, and wet cloth.
32. Tell me I didn't feel that bad.
33. She dropped everything.
34. Usually, when she was home. But if she picked me up from school sick, she would drop me off at home and go back to work.
35. Tomato soup and grilled cheese in bed.
36. She wasn't home to take care of me.
37. She gave me medicine, made me food, gave me movies to watch, and helped me when I needed it.
38. Threw me meds and told me to suck it up.
39. Gave me water and special treats.
40. Made sure she gave medicine, drinks, and I was comfortable.
41. Caring, loving, and stayed with me. Made me comfortable and made sure I did what the Doc ordered. She still does.
42. Took me to the doctor, made sure my meds were on time with correct dosage. She kept me warm, clean, hydrated, and fed. She sent me to my Nana when she tired of this. I got peenewmonia (that's what she called it. LOL) every winter. It was weeks of caring for me at that time.

43. She was amazing, this woman worked three jobs and still had time to cook and clean while her health was dwindling. She would make sure I was warm, fed, medication. Then again, she did go to school for nursing; she has heart.
44. With care and love.
45. She cuddled me but gave me the space I demanded.
46. She use to rub Vicks on my chest and make a tent on my crib when I got the croup.
47. I wasn't her favorite so my dad took care of me.
48. Soup, popsicles, and lots of snuggles.
49. Stayed in bed and forced to eat.
50. My mom was pregnant thirteen times, and each child always got time with her.
51. Stayed by my side and sang to me.
52. She could be tender and doting.
53. Lovingly until you tried to milk it.
54. She made the couch up with a pillow and blanket. She and my dad would anoint me with oil and lay their hands on me and pray for me.
55. She cooked for me, sang to me, and played with my hair.
56. Made me hot tea and soup, kept me wrapped in a blanket.
57. She stayed home and made me soup.
58. Whenever I was really little, I loved to be lightly tickled on my arm, and she would do that until I feel asleep.
59. Telling me to rest and making me food and getting me medication. (2)
60. She's a doctor, so she would mostly tell me I'm fine and to get over it.
61. When I was little, she was supportive and nurturing. As I got older, she was expecting more independence from us.
62. Would bring me medicine and tell me to stay my room so my siblings wouldn't get sick.
63. Warm hugs, medicine, and lots of laughter.
64. She took care of me medically but also with love, tenderness, and extra love and attention.
65. Did not get "that" sick.

66. Nursing me back with medicine and love.
67. She taught me to persevere.
68. She sent me to my grandparent's to get better.
69. Prayer.
70. Soup, bed rest, and doctor's appointment.
71. She was the most loving when I was sick, really loving and tender. It made me enjoy being sick, and I found myself faking sickness to get this loving attention.
72. I was definitely cuddled when I was sick, and I'm not complaining, although it kind of ruined me for being sick as an adult because I have to take care of myself.
73. I don't remember getting sick. But when I had surgery, she was right there to help me with anything I needed.

Now it's your turn to answer.

When you were sick, how did she take care of you?

_____

_____

_____

_____

_____

_____

_____

_____

_____

_____

_____

_____

_____

_____

_____

_____

_____

_____

_____

_____

_____

_____

_____

_____

Chapter 9

If You Could Wrap a Blanket Around You in the Color and/or the Texture of Your Mom, What Would It Look and Feel Like? (A hug)

I hug my girls a lot, so I can't imagine them looking at me when they are in their forties and saying I didn't hug them enough or never showed my love. I really just can't. I can say I probably have smothered them in hugs.

One of my girls sent me a meme that had the word smother in it. She said, "See, Mom, you can't help it because mother is actually a part of the word *smother*! LOL.

Thanks, kiddo! You gave me permission with your acknowledgement! The rule we have (I made. LOL) is no one leaves the house without a hug. Even the girls' friends know that "rule." I tease about the eye rolls and then the smiles they share. I don't want to ever have the regret that the one time they left the house, I forgot to hug them. And now, when the kids are not home, away at school with their families, I just want to hug them. My heart hurts a bit that I can't every day. I try not to cry when I miss them. Fail. Don't tell them.

I know they are aware. "See you later" gets harder these days. Thank God for the memories of snuggles on the couch during movie time or story times.

Just writing this, and knowing what is coming, is tough! It *sucks*! I have already listened to "God Help Me" three times. I want slam the laptop closed and *run*! So I listen to this song to do what is

77

expected and needed. Do you need to stop reading and go listen to it? I will be here when you get back. Probably still listening myself for a few more times.

So I stepped away. Not for long. Just long enough to go upstairs with my phone and headphones to listen to that song, with no distractions: To worship and give all to God. To really listen to the words, to feel them, to understand them, to use the words and meaning. To go forward, to write, to share and heal.

There is physical pain with this one. A pain in my heart as if it really were breaking in two pieces. I can't imagine not hugging my kids daily when they were little. Of course, they were children so they got in trouble. But even after, that how could I not hug them?

I didn't get good morning hugs or any before I left for school. Occasionally, when I got home, but that is because I reached out to her. At bedtime, yes. It wasn't like a real hug. Sort of like a ritual or leading the cows to slaughter. We would line up to hug her and my father goodnight. We would get and give a quick pat on the back and get it over with. Each one of us said, "Love you, Mom, love you, Dad," and out we went. They always seemed to be in their room. I hated that room, the smell and the color. There is so much deep, deep pain about that room and the hatred for it that is for another time and place.

When this question was given to me, I thought how insane is this. Why would I get such an odd way of asking if we got a hug from our mother? I did but not always, not every day. It was a hug, so I thought. I never knew there could be more ways than a few to describe how a hug felt, until reading responses from you. To be honest, I thought that this was going to be a stupid, unnecessary question. Who cares about a hug? You either got them or didn't. But it is so very much more than just merely a question of did your mother figure hug you or not.

One of the first thoughts after seeing how important it was to ask was how it felt. I had to put myself mentally back there. Back in that house on Canterbury Street, I can still picture the layout of the house. Each room, and who it belonged to and where the trash cans in the kitchen, were kept. Even the house phone, the kind with a rotary dial and where it hung right beside the back glass sliding double doors on the left.

Like I said before, yes, I got hugs. I think we can call them that. The best hug I got, I can totally remember well. But before I tell of that hug, I have to give the reason I got it.

My parents didn't get along, and when my father was going through his power hungry ways (one time of many), basically, my mother was in a moment of "I'm done." He couldn't handle it, so he said we had to choose, him or her. And if you knew him, we sided with him. We literally took a vote of who wanted her gone. He told us before she was in the room that she was sick and didn't want us right then. We needed to make her leave; we needed to vote her gone. So he gathered us; we didn't know she had already decided to leave for a few days. One of her parents were on their way over to get her. We had no idea how or what the plan already was. As I sit here, I realize that all he wanted to do was put salt in her already torn-open wounds. What better way to do that than have your five children hurt you too? My father asked each one of us if she was to stay or go. Each of her five children, ages seven to sixteen, said, "She has to go away."

I still remember the look on her face, the pain in my heart, and the lump in my throat. I was nine. I would be ten in less than two months. I only know my age because it was the year the movie *E.T.* came out in theaters. My grandparent didn't even pull into the driveway, just along the curb. Honked, she left. We didn't hug. She just said goodbye and walked out the door, closing it after her. I ran to my bedroom to watch her out my window. She didn't even look back. Had she, I think I would have wanted to run out after her. I don't remember who was driving the little green car. I just focused on her walking away from me, nothing, just gone. I know, what was she supposed to say? We told her to leave. I didn't want her to go! I hated her; I loved her. She didn't fight for us again! My mother was gone for a few weeks. I honestly do not remember anything about that time, except she was gone. She left in May. I know we had school. I know we had to have watched TV, been outside, had homework, ate food; I don't remember anything at all! One day, he said she was coming home, and then she was there. She was smiling and laughing. And hugging me! She didn't let go right away. It was the warmest hug I had ever gotten. Not even being sick or getting hurt or being scared got me that type of hug! I even got a kiss on the forehead. A warm hug, *wow*, a moment in time I can go back to and see and feel her love through a wonderfully warm hug.

I would like to leave it there and walk away from this chapter now. That is not going to happen yet.

I will tell you that there was not another hug like that again. I ended up being angry at her when she started talking about all the great and fun stuff she did while she was away from us. Going to see *E. T.* was the first. I honestly did not watch that movie until I was about fifteen. Every time I thought about it, I would get angry again. Even now, I find myself being a bit jacked because of her leaving. Every time I hear the name of the movie, I think back to a hot second in my life that was chaos.

Maybe if that had not been the only time I received a hug like that, I wouldn't have been so angry and bitter. I know that every hug after that was like a gray wool blanket, like the ones they show in the old war movies. They serve their purpose but not liked at all. That's my opinion anyways. I don't like wool. I think it is scratchy and ugly. The only use for it is to be hung over a cold drafty window at night in the dead of winter.

A child *should not* have to work for a warm hug from their mother! They should know that in the arms of that woman, they are safe, warm, protected, wanted, and loved. And if for a moment, my children think I smother them with hugs then good. Because they will also never doubt that it is a hug that was given freely, and they never had to work for it, not a hassle to give, always a joy to receive, and safe, warm, protection. They are wanted and loved so very, very much! I can't wait to see them so I can squeeze them tight!! Okay, I lied, maybe "smother" them a little.

And now I will show you the most excellent way.
If I speak in the tongues of men and of angels,
but not love, I am only a resounding gong or a

clanging cymbal. If I have the gift of prophecy and can fathom all mysteries and all knowledge, and if I have a faith that can move mountains, but have not love, I am nothing. If I give all I possess to the poor and surrender my body to the flames, but have not love, I gain nothing. Love is patient, love is kind. It does not envy, it does not boast, it is not proud. It is not rude, it is not self-seeking, it is not easily angered, it keeps no record of wrongs. Love does not delight in evil but rejoices with the truth, it always protects, always trusts, always hopes, always perseveres. Love never fails. But where there are prophecies, they will cease; where there are tongues, they will be stilled; where there is knowledge, it will pass away. For we know in part and we prophesy in part, but when perfection comes, the imperfect disappears. When I was a child, I talked like a child, I thought like a child, I reasoned like a child. When I became a man, I put childish ways behind me. Now we see but a poor reflection as in a mirror; then we shall see face to face. Now I know in part; then I shall know fully, even as I am fully known. And now these three remain: faith, hope and love. But the greatest of these is love. (1 Corinthians 13:1–13, NIV)

I feel like this is how hugs should be, full of love and compassion, always be full of love.

Responses

1. Heavy quilt.
2. Green prickly pear cactus.
3. It would be pink or mauve, warm, durable and very strong but soft, maybe a little worn at the edge from much use.
4. A white plush throw.
5. An afghan.
6. A teal wool blanket. Would not wrap up in it, I am allergic to wool.
7. Warm and soft, big and fluffy like the ones I make.
8. A heavy wet multicolored afghan.
9. The softest and warmest sheep wool around!
10. It would be green, her favorite color, a light green. It would look like a quilt.
11. Soft, warm, and blue.
12. Fleeced, light purple and warm and secure.
13. Soft but firm, brown and tan, very warm and heavy.
14. Soft but heavy.
15. Would be fleece and pink. (5)
16. Warm chocolate and fleecy.
17. Like a baby's skin.
18. Blue, soft, warm and safe.
19. Suffocating.
20. Heavy, rough, and purple.
21. Gray fleece.
22. Blue fuzzy fleece. (7)
23. Soft and holy.
24. Red and furry. (4)
25. It would be a blue knitted blanket. With that, there are holes and sometimes mistakes, but it is all connected together.
26. Light-blue super soft cotton.
27. It would be a purple, thick and super soft blanket that makes you feel so comfortable and loved.
28. *Safe.*

29. Honestly, my mom tried her best but had issues due to her childhood and divorce. I wish she had sought therapy. The blanket would be rough but warm.
30. Warm fleece. (2)
31. Red, her favorite color, and it would be soft and warm.
32. A big, cozy brownish purple, not fleece but softer.
33. It would be blue because that's her favorite color, and it would be fluffy and soft because my mom is never harsh or mean.
34. Soft-aqua fleece.
35. It would be a plain blanket, nothing fancy or bright but warm and cozy.
36. It would be like a blue (favorite color) squishy ball. We pick on her about her being short and round.
37. Pastels and soft. (3)
38. Dark red-purple brown color and wool.
39. Mint green, soft, fluffy, and warm.
40. Fuzzy blanket because it was worn.
41. Purple and soft.
42. Black and scratchy.
43. Soft lavender.
44. Bluish gray, falling apart and absorbing into itself and scratchy.
45. It would be like a lovie that is old and worn but the most comfortable and warming piece of blanket.
46. Rough brown and wiry feeling.
47. Fleece, warm but everything sticks to it.
48. Itchy.
49. Ewww, yuck! An itchy, rough, woolen one with soft pastel colors.
50. This makes me want to cry, and I'm not sure why. The blanket would be blue and maybe some purples and reds, even pink. Because this woman has been through so much, and while I know a lot of people had a hard life, this woman is a prime example. She still raised us kids on her own without anyone or assistance. We were not always close until these

past six years or so. I love her so much. The material on this blanket would be soft for her heart, lace, and a bit rough on the edges for all her hard work. And smell like flowers because she's the sweetest woman I know. The hug, the hug would be strong for all she's been through and passed on to me so I may pass it on to my daughters. Materials, leather for the roughness on her hands for all her hard work, baby-soft down, lace, and love.

51. Pink and soft, an angora.
52. A warm, soft yet firm blanket.
53. Soft like cashmere and it would be blue like the sky.
54. A clean sheet from the clothes line.
55. Gray.
56. Soft with flowers and angels on it.
57. Black wool.
58. Smell like lilacs and silky light blue.
59. Soft and like a patchwork quilt.
60. It would be pink and soft at first, then scratchy like wool.
61. Purple and warm or fuzzy, like the good fuzzy blankets (a heated one).
62. Bright warm and soft.
63. Cold.
64. Dark-blue, knitted, thick and fuzzy and very heavy.
65. Wrinkled but warm.
66. It would be purple and smell like her. Purple because she deserves honor. It would be warm and fuzzy because that is what she loves to curl up under.
67. Yellow and feel soft.
68. Wool blanket.
69. Purple, warm, and squishy.
70. Pink, soft, warm, and secure.
71. Thin and short.
72. Soft like a fleece. (2)
73. Ocean blue, soft, and warm.
74. A queen-sized purple, blue, and green quilt.
75. Soft, fuzzy, big blanket.

76. Sky blue, orange, calming like heaven.
77. Soft, fluffy, yellow.
78. A blue fleece blanket. It would cling to my body like a second skin. But it is a breathable fabric. It would be extremely soft and supremely comforting.
79. Loosely knitted.
80. Ha-ha, well really, that depends on her mood or what part of my life we are talking about.
81. A very fluffy, soft camouflage, she has always been there for me as God is and protective and loving, no matter my choices and consequences.
82. It would be very soft on one side, a little itchy on the other side, and it would be tie-dyed.
83. Sandpaper—my mother was hardly ever a soft person. Dark colors, she was a very controlling and hard person. I always thought she was never happy, and she didn't want us to be either.
84. White, super soft, and fluffy. The kind you can bury your face into.
85. Burlap with itchy wool and briars.
86. A red wool blanket because she likes the color red and because wool is very uncomfortable at times and not pleasant.
87. Beige and a little scratchy.
88. It would be purple and soft as a cotton ball.
89. There is a wool like blanket in our house. It reminds me of her for a few reasons: it's always been around; it's big and warm but a little scratchy. (1) My mom has always been there. There was never a time I needed her that she wasn't physically available to me somehow. (2) Let's be honest, mom hugs are kind of the best. (3) Sometimes, she can be a little rough around the edges. Wool is very, very warm but a little scratchy. My mom has always cared deeply for us (that was never a question), but sometimes, I think I felt a little invaded. There was a decent amount of stuff I didn't want to share but felt forced to. I noticed that when

my sister was a teenager, my sister hid everything, and my mom needed to know what was going on and would find the answer any way she could. I've always valued personal space, and growing up, I felt like I wasn't allowed to keep anything from her.

90. Rough cotton at one end, getting a little softer at the other end.

Now it's your turn to answer.

If you could wrap a blanket around you, in the color and or the texture of your mom, what would it look like or feel like?

_____

_____

_____

_____

_____

_____

_____

_____

_____

_____

_____

_____

_____

_____

_____

_____

_____

_____

_____

_____

_____

_____

_____

_____

_____

Chapter 10

A Tradition She Started When You Were a Child That You Still Do

When I think of tradition, I feel like it should absolutely be a most positive, wonderful experience. As I am sure, most of you do as well. But do we really appreciate those things that we carry on with, or is it simply out of habit that it is done? Is it more like a ritual that must be done because the generation before you did it?

I know some things we continue is a way to hold on to the memory of the one who started the tradition. I get that. There are people in my life that I would probably continue things just because they did it. To hang on to moments in time when they were with us.

There is one thing that I can remember when I was a kid. And because it is a good thing, I want to talk about that in a minute. I didn't give you guys the option for this part, but what about those things that should mean something to you as you are older with a family that you just don't want to do? As we were growing up, we sat at the table together for all meals: Breakfast, during the week, at the table together. Lunch, if we were home during the summer, at the table together. Lunch was mostly just the five kids. But dinner was almost every single night at the kitchen table. Most of the time, all seven of us sat there together.

Everything happened at that table. So much pain happened at that table: My father molesting me in the early mornings while he drank coffee and sat in his blue long johns. Yelling, screaming, threats of abuse to come, drinking all night with his friends. Lectures that would continue late into the night as you tried to stay awake.

My mother always wanted us at the table together. Most meals were calm with little to no fighting. It was moments where there was no competition among the kids. Nothing was expected of you, except you eat your meal. If you didn't eat right away, you could sit for hours. If you didn't like what was fixed and you didn't finish it, then it would be served to you at the next meal. And it was not heated even if it was meant to be. Ever eat cold liver and onions with nasty green beans or horrid lima beans, nasty canned spinach? Yep, I gag now just thinking about it. So why do I write about a tradition that I couldn't stand and one I rarely follow now? There are a few reasons. When I first got to this chapter, I thought about how many ways can I write the word *nothing* all over the page. How many sizes, how many styles and directions, and how many times could I get that one word on one page. A lot.

I just happen to be sitting at my dining room table now as I work. This is where I do all my writing, scheduling, card writing, research, or anything on the laptop. It is covered now with note-books, blank and filled in packets of the book questions. Pens, high-lighters, paperclips, water bottle, a few Bibles, dictionary, calendars, a large box of tissues. Ideas for another tattoo, pieces of paper with tons of scripture I wrote down during the sermons at church, never knowing when they will be needed or applied to the moment I am in.

There is no room to place a plate or any other dishes, except for a coffee cup. It's not that I have a small table; it is very nice and large. With the leaf in it, it seats eight comfortably. We could probably get ten around it. This table is only a year or two old, and I love it. I'm even the one who picked it out.

Do you know what I saw when I chose it? The only times we would need this many chairs would be Thanksgiving dinner, Christmas dinner, and Easter dinner. At first, I thought it would be big enough to make cookies and such, but there are grooves in it, and I have the kitchen island for that. The other reason I wanted this one was for the six-thousand-piece puzzle I have. It's just wide enough for that though, LOL. But it takes too long to work on, and I needed it for a holiday dinner.

So why am I making a big deal about a table that the main reason we purchased was for three meals? Because I find it sad that some things I have a very difficult time moving away from in my memories. When the kids were smaller, we ate at the table. We talked about their day at school and talked about the day and the next day plans. We used it to make cookies and paint and color. We played with play dough and laughed a lot. We cried at the table for others and our own struggles. What I realize is that the pain at the table as a child, the threats from both parents, the stress and frustration has to be dealt with in order for my table to be inviting now. I can sit here and work and write and plan because it is only me. I am in charge at this time, of my time, at my table, my rules. No one will bully here; no one will tower over another with threats; and no fear will be felt because of another person's control and abusive behavior.

I say that now because I am not the same person I used to be. I was like that angry parent before Jesus saved my life. Maybe it is guilt that I was like my mother in ways. We had a smaller table when my oldest daughter was eighteen. She thought she knew it all, and well, I didn't handle it well. I had a temper that would make my husband leave the room in disgust. This smaller table got flipped with whatever was on it toward her when she made a choice I didn't like. I thought I was trying to protect her from what she wanted to do. If I had handled it differently, maybe it would have gone another direction. Then again, maybe not. I thought I was fighting for her in that moment; I was fighting against her. Needless to say, she freaked out as I would have and moved out to be with that boyfriend. It didn't last long, and she did move home. But I did not handle it right. I feel like the way I acted is how my mother might have acted if I had stayed in that house. Then again, maybe not. I blew it, I do know that. I think that is something I needed to convey here, that I blew it multiple times like my mother did. My oldest is now twenty-eight, and it has been a long road of getting it wrong and learning how to do it right. I fail often but not as often or as bad as I used to.

My dear brothers and sisters, take note of this:
Everyone should be quick to listen, slow to speak

and slow to become angry, because human anger does not produce the righteousness that God desires. Therefore, get rid of all moral filth and the evil that is so prevalent and humbly accept the word planted in you, which can save you. (James 1:19–21, NIV)

Now that I spent time on why I won't follow one tradition, let's go to one I do. So I grew up mostly in Eugene, Oregon. And I don't remember getting as much snow there as we do now in Pennsylvania. When it would snow as a kid, I loved it! That has never changed; my love for the snow has been as long as I can remember. I don't care for how cold it gets here, but it is home and has plenty of snow during the winter.

I can't remember how old we were when this first started, just that we were on Canterbury Street. It was around nine or so, and we were supposed to be getting ready for bed I believe. It started snowing! And it was coming down fast with big snowflakes! My father took the dogs outside and across the street to run in the empty parking lot. Our mother and myself and another sibling or two took our socks off and ran out the back door to the patio! I can still feel the cold, wet feeling on my feet. Shocked that my mother was acting like a kid and having fun. We were only out for a few shorts moments, but those moments have always brought me happiness when I see the snow start to fall. For those first seconds, no matter where I am when it starts to snow, takes me back to laughter and rushing to get our bare feet in the cold snow. Then the hurrying to get back in and get our feet warm again. And even as the warmth takes over, the smile and laughter doesn't stop right away. Those silly things and times in your life that you don't realize you will carry with you as an adult. When you think that all was horrible in your life, God reminds you that not every second of every day or week, month or year were horrible. He gives you a second to see some joy when life was normally tough and difficult.

For the longest time, I thought it was just my sister and I that ran out in the snow. As I sat here before I began writing this section,

I thought, am I wrong? Did my mother not go out with us? Did she not start this? Then for a few minutes, I thought that my head might explode because I was trying to force her into a memory she wasn't in. I even prayed God how can she not be in this. Have I been wrong all this time? Was I just placing her there so I could have something to write about since I posed that question to you? Did I lie to the girls and tell them their grandmother started this tradition we have done since they were little? Did she go across the road to the empty parking lot with my father and the dogs while we snuck outside? I shake my head no. She was there. Maybe just for a moment, but she was there. She loves the snow. Of course it was her too. The snow can bring out the kid in anyone!

So yes, we continue it. The first snow, we take our socks off, run outside, and run around in bare feet. Freezing and cold, screaming and laughing, living and being like children. And as when I was a child, running back into the house with re freezing cold feet, laughing at each other with smiles on our face, just like I did.

I love those moments with the kids.

With them growing up and not always home with the first snow, it's hard. I feel like I'm missing out. One has her own family about fifteen minutes away. The youngest daughter is away at college, two-and-a-half hours away. So this year, we were on the phone and ran outside in our bare feet! Laughing on the phone in the snow, feeling those same emotions as I did years before! And we decided, if there is snow on the ground and we are not all together, we will get on the phone, take our socks off, running outside barefooted to feel the cold, wet, freezing snow on our feet. Rush in to get warm again as we laugh and carry on. That is a tradition worth doing and keeping it going; I hope they carry on with their children.

And when they see that first or last snow begin to fall, they smile and memories of joy flood their minds, and they smile.

I am grateful for a moment my mother let her guard down because it became a memory and tradition that as long as I am able, I will do. And now, when I do it, I can think of her and smile. Maybe next year, on that first snow, I will have to add her to the conference call for a moment of laughter and joy. Maybe I will make two calls that next time and have a time with just me and Mom, and hopefully, there will be snow on the ground for her too.

I really hope one day, my granddaughters call me when they are on their own for that conference call of first snow joy!

I wonder how many of you will do this when it snows again? LOL.

If you think about it, you might as well do it! Allow a moment to be childlike again, laugh, and live a little. One snow at a time!

Guess what?

There is snow on the ground!

Responses

1. Christmas jammies and coloring books.
2. Putting an orange in your Christmas stocking.
3. Having dinner as a family almost every night. (3)
4. Chores on a certain day of the week.
5. She had glass trees; she filled them up with candy every Christmas. My two sisters and I have glass trees, and we fill them up.
6. Prayed the Armor of God on us every single day.
7. Making Christmas ornaments.
8. Shamrock shakes at McDonalds every year. That's just one of many.
9. A lot! Her mom was called home to God when she was young. Her stepmom wasn't into traditions, so she started a lot of her own when she had me and my siblings.
10. Baking Christmas cookies. (2)
11. Christmas Eve celebration with family. (3)
12. Have sauerkraut every New Year.
13. Making something homemade for the Christmas tree.
14. Decorating and baking long before the holiday. Not so much baking since the kids are grown.
15. Holiday gathering with the kids.
16. Making homemade ice cream.
17. Wearing slippers on Christmas Eve.
18. Holiday dinners. (3)
19. Family decorates Christmas tree together.
20. New Year's Day together.
21. Saturday morning breakfast.
22. Separating out Christmas presents on Christmas Eve.
23. New Christmas PJs for kids.
24. Family gatherings. (2)
25. Pray. (2)
26. Baking pumpkin rolls.

27. She continued traditions from her parents, and we still continue them. One would be Polish Christmas Eve dinner with oplatki (Christmas wafer).
28. Sending cards to nonfamily members just because. I send cards to our churches college students so they know they are important.
29. Christmas, having a large dinner shared with family and friends and open your home to someone who has no place to go.
30. Open all gifts on Christmas Eve, expect those from Santa.
31. Beans on New Year's Day.
32. Decorating for Christmas. (2)
33. The way we do Thanksgiving and Christmas.
34. Every holiday, the entire family comes over for dinner.
35. Watching Macy's Thanksgiving parade.
36. Make special food during the holidays.
37. Sundays at Grandma's.
38. Root beer floats on Christmas morning.
39. Zoo trips.
40. Open one present on Christmas Eve. (3)
41. Eat pizza for lunch on Christmas.
42. Getting away on weekends for family fun.
43. All traditions of each holiday, she also taught me to never forget those who had been called home before us. Go and decorate their grave, visit them, and be "with" them to share their memories with others.
44. Sing from your heart.
45. Prayer before meals, even though my children are getting older. For the longest time, sing "You Are My Sunshine" even if they giggle at me.
46. Birthday cake.
47. Yard sales.
48. Life-saver books in Christmas stockings.
49. Beans and fried potatoes.
50. Hunt Easter baskets.
51. Prayers before bed.

52. Putting icicles on Christmas tree on Christmas Eve.
53. A family story.
54. Filling Easter basket for my son every year even though he is grown.
55. Look nice for church.
56. Reading the story of Christmas from the Bible, Christmas Eve.
57. Find the pickle on the Christmas tree.
58. Iced tea with dinner.
59. Playing (and beating me) in tennis.
60. Ham pot pie noodles as a family affair.
61. Kissing goodnight.
62. Little things on holidays—cinnamon rolls Christmas morning. Traveling as little as possible when the kids were young to give them a holiday at home with family rather than spending all day in a car.
63. Help strangers any way possible.
64. Listen to Christmas songs while drinking hot chocolate and decorating the Christmas tree.
65. Wintertime homemade ice cream family get together.
66. Make sure your children know that you're always there for them and that family is important.
67. Can't take down the tree until after sauerkraut.
68. Love your children.
69. Telling us a story about Jack and Manory, which I told my kids.
70. Letting the kids pick a new Christmas ornament for the tree every year.
71. Sunday dinners.
72. Buying a Christmas tree ornament for my children for Christmas every year.
73. Attending church.
74. Baking cookies for Christmas and making pumpkin rolls for Thanksgiving.
75. Keeping in touch with family, I call my sister in New York twice a day every day.

76. Christmas morning breakfast eggs.
77. During the first snowfall of winter (when the snow actually lays and sticks to the ground), she and my sister and I run out in the snow in our bare feet. Since being away at college, I've still done it if ever I'm not home with her. My friend's think I'm insane.
78. Hiding the kids' Easter baskets.

Now it's your turn to answer.

A tradition she started when you were a child that you still do?

_____

_____

_____

_____

_____

_____

_____

_____

_____

_____

_____

_____

_____

_____

_____

_____

_____

_____

_____

_____

_____

_____

_____

_____

_____

_____

_____

Chapter 11

A Tradition You Started with Your Family

When I was a kid, we would go to my grandparent's house Christmas day. We would see uncles and aunts and cousins, open a few presents, grab a mini candy cane or two off the fake tree, and have dinner. It was a big turkey, stuffing, mashed potatoes, gravy, disgusting green beans, and dessert, chocolate pie! Others as well but chocolate was my favorite. I think I said that earlier too. I was twelve the last time I lived with my birth parents. I know that every year, we went to the grandparent's house. There were two years I know we didn't go. One year, I was in a foster home during Christmas. And the other Christmas time I remember not going there is the year I was taken from them for the last time. That was December 17 at 7:30 in the evening on a Saturday. We were decorating a live Christmas tree, with the big bulbs. I don't recall any other decorations, but I wouldn't know that year because the tree wasn't finished before the police showed up. I have no idea where the tree came from, who brought it over or even setting it in a stand. I just remember we were putting lights on when there was a knock on the door. I can recall that whole day from wake up to not being able to sleep until around 3:00 a.m. the next morning.

Basically, one of my sisters had run away because my father threatened to kill her. I knew that morning before school, she wasn't coming home. All day, I sat in school wondering if I would ever see her again, or alive for that matter. I did as she told me and kept my mouth shut. She did tell me that she would see me again. I didn't believe her. She was gone for a week I think when that knock came at the door.

She saved my life in that moment. I think she knows that. As hard as it was that day, she gave me a chance to breathe.

She has always been my sibling hero! She was out there for days alone and got the courage to ask for help. She told them the truth; they believed her! We went to the same group home and, from there, separated into different foster homes. I don't know why, they just did it that way. It was a horrible struggle. See, when we went in to that foster care home, it was called a shelter home. A temporary place as they tried to figure out what was next for us. I think they separated us because we were too much to handle together. She would get mad at the rules and the fact we were not allowed contact with anyone, not even school friends. Then I would get mad too, and I think they just didn't know what to do with us. Maybe I wouldn't be so hard to deal with if we were separated. She was the reason I was safe! Why couldn't I stay wherever she was? It is crazy that I can recall moments and days and dates of a long time ago but can't remember the exact date I quit drinking and using drugs. I know the month, not the date.

I remember what I got that year for Christmas while in the shelter home thirty-three years ago. A doll someone made that was supposed to look like a cabbage patch doll. I still have it, the one I got from a stranger. I also received a big full-size handmade quilt. That thing was torn and mended so many times. The quilt lasted roughly twenty-two years with me. It was so tattered that when our German shepherd died, I wrapped her up in it, and we buried her.

What does all of this have to do with traditions we start? Simply, Christmas was such a difficult time after that last day with my biological family that something had to change. I loved the snow when it came. I love Christmas trees all lit up. I love the smell of a big Douglas fir in the house! The colors of Christmas make me happy. I got tired of being sad and hurting the month of December. It's not like I could remember all the holidays with my family, so why not make it my own. Christmas was going to be my time, my holiday, and my way of having joy.

There are traditions that we do and have done for the last twenty-two years. Some have been adjusted as far as when, like getting the Christmas tree for example. We used to get it the first weekend of December because it fell on brat's birthday. Brat is one of her nicknames. When she struggled for a while and wasn't around, I changed getting the tree to black Friday. She went with us a few years ago; it was great having her a part of this tradition again!

For twenty-two years, we have taken the kids, and that includes any of the foster kids we had over the years, and we would go to the tree farm. We would walk to the "perfect" spot or get a wagon ride. As soon as the journey started, the kids and John would make jokes about how long it would take Mom to find just the right tree. We normally spent two to two-and-a-half hours from start when we pulled in to the farm, to finish when we loaded the tree or trees onto the vehicle. The first year we went, our Panda was six months old. Snuggled up in her snowsuit with a blanket around her, we walked out through the field to get the tree.

This year, she didn't need a snow suit, but they still laughed at me for how long picking out the tree took. It has to be the right size, big and fluffy! I always think they might be too short, but then we get it in the house and it's huge! I love big green Douglas fir trees.

So then there is getting the tree in the stand, and the next day or evening, it is decorated. I have a favorite Christmas CD of Kenny and Dolly. So we crank it up and decorate the tree. And it takes way longer than the CD is so we just pick random music and continue to decorate with decorations that we have had for twenty plus years, with a few new ones every year. I still have the homemade ones from when the kids were in school.

The last part of decorating the tree is putting on the tinsel. We get strands in our hands, toss it up, and blow, so it hits where we want it. Yes, it sounds silly, but it is fun and we laugh a lot.

This year was a little tough because of the kid's school schedules. We had time to get the trees but had to decide to decorate or bring a few of the grandkids over to make and decorate Christmas cookies. Well, we picked making sugar cookies and listening to the Christmas and other music. I enjoyed the extra little hands in the cookie dough this year! And yes, Grammy has eyes in the back of her head to see the dough they were eating. A giggle almost every time kind of gave it away too!

I will say decorating a big old Christmas tree by myself was not enjoyable. At least, thanks to video chat, they could see the finished work. Every year, they tell me how crazy I am and that the tree is huge.

I did miss one tradition before getting the tree. Thanksgiving evening, we watch *A Christmas Carol*, one of the many versions! We will watch them until the New Year.

Christmas morning, John reads the story from the Bible of Jesus's birth. Then he and our youngest son deliver a load of wood, and I make homemade cinnamon rolls. This year, Panda helped and we made homemade icing.

I know that kids grow up and make their own paths with traditions of their own choosing. I would love to continue these events as long as possible. I loved having some of the grandkids here to see how their mom and aunt had fun. My heart is full in moments like this, when I see the looks on the girls' faces as they dance around the kitchen singing together. Another moment when all was right in my world!

"I praise you for remembering me in everything and for holding to the traditions just as I passed them on to you" (1 Corinthians 11:2, NIV).

"So then, brothers, stand firm and hold to the traditions that you were taught by us, either by our spoken word or by our letter" (2 Thessalonians 2:15, ESV).

Responses

1. Christmas jammies and coloring book.
2. Ignoring each other.
3. I still put an orange in Toby's stocking.
4. Teaching my daughter to do chores, to clean her room.
5. Watching my two younger nieces open their Christmas gifts.
6. Divulging all information about our lives around the supper table.
7. Making Christmas ornaments.
8. Shamrock shakes.
9. Make sure that my son and I have a "family" day once a week.
10. Christmas cookies and planting flowers at the cemetery.
11. Have sauerkraut every New Year.
12. Letting the kids decorate the tree.
13. Christmas coloring books.
14. Family first.
15. Taking them to church when I can get them to go.
16. Singing a song with my kids at bedtime.
17. Holiday dinners.
18. Holiday baking.(2)
19. Pizza and movie night. (2)
20. Sunday morning breakfast.
21. Making candies and cookies for Christmas.
22. John and I get our picture taken in front of the Christmas tree at the candle light service every Christmas eve.
23. Christmas Eve boxes.
24. Christmas family get together.
25. Making up and telling stories and singing.
26. Church every Sunday.(2)
27. Saying grace before meals together.
28. New pajamas for Christmas Eve.
29. Gift exchange between just us on Christmas Eve after others have gone home.

30. Feeding reindeer before bed on Christmas Eve.
31. Loving and hugging.
32. Movie and game nights.
33. Bedtime prayer time.
34. Christmas Eve no lights, just candles. No electronics, just family time.
35. Movie dates with my kids.
36. Love.
37. Giving each of my children a song that is just theirs and mine.
38. Sharing the day's highs and lows at dinner.
39. Open house Thanksgiving.
40. Overnight trips to places the kids want to go.
41. Open one present on Christmas Eve.
42. Every holiday, we spend time doing crafts.
43. How little things in life mean a lot. That worship is important in our daily lives, that our parents won't be her on earth forever and that love never fails.
44. Always stand with family.
45. Never say bye, it's too final. Same as my mother taught us, it's see you later! Try to eat together and do not clean or shop on Sundays.
46. Gifts.
47. Meals at the table.
48. Pray.
49. Decorating for the holidays together.
50. Hunt Easter baskets.
51. Family holidays.
52. Getting together Christmas Eve.
53. Praying as a family. (2)
54. Always together on Christmas and doing a PKD (Polycystic Kidney Disease) walk for a cure.
55. What happens at Grammys stays at Grammys.
56. Handpicking our Christmas tree and cutting it down ourselves.
57. Pot pie at Christmas.

58. Hold hands and pray before every meal.
59. Cutting down our Christmas tree the kids picked.
60. Saying I love you when we talk, meet, or leave one another.
61. Love people, treasure your time with them, avoid drama.
62. Christmas Eve new jammies, movie, hot chocolate, and camping.
63. Having a church that's my family.
64. Stuffing balls for Thanksgiving and Christmas.
65. No Santa. My husband and I gave our children three gifts every year for Christmas to represent each gift brought by the wise men.
66. Telling the Christmas story.
67. Purchasing Christmas PJs for my grandchildren to wear on Christmas Eve.
68. Twenty-five books for Christmas, opening one every night until Christmas Eve.
69. Serving others, respecting all, and helping others in whatever manner we can help!
70. Being and saying nice things to each other.
71. Every Thanksgiving, everyone speaks at the dinner table about what they are most thankful for.
72. Try to do movie night with all the kids. Christmas Day everyone at my house and Easter eggs on Easter.
73. Singing happy birthday to Jesus Christmas morning, reading together, cooking together, and decorating the Christmas tree together.
74. Going black Friday shopping with my daughters.
75. Thanksgiving at my aunts.
76. Camping.

Now it's your turn to answer.

A tradition you started with your family?

_____
_____
_____
_____
_____
_____
_____
_____
_____
_____
_____
_____
_____
_____
_____
_____
_____
_____
_____
_____
_____
_____
_____
_____
_____
_____
_____
_____
_____
_____

Chapter 12

Do You Know Her Favorite Bible Verse

Yes, I know her favorite Bible verse. It is John 3:16: "For God so loved the world that he gave his one and only Son, that whoever believes in him shall not perish but have eternal life." I did not know it until a few months ago. I simply called and asked her. Was it cheating? Yes, I will say it was. When I say it was an act of simply calling, it's a little more than that. Every time I think about calling her, I get anxious. When I dial, I continue to be anxious, but in those few short moments of hearing it ring, I write the ending to the phone call. Like she won't answer or she will not be nice, it will be like pulling teeth trying to have a decent conversation, so on and so on. When I talked to her last, I wrote the wrong ending again. Apparently, she can't hear very well and won't wear her hearing aid. Something I didn't know she even had. So when she actually answered the phone, she hung up when I said hello. So you can imagine my brain worked overtime. So I called back, said "Hello, hello, hello, it's Christy." Click. I was jacked. I got so mad and so upset that I cried. I told my husband it's not like I wanted to talk to her anyway. And that I was tired of trying. Yes, I know that was a lie. It was a way I tried to protect my heart again from disappointment. Fail. About five minutes later, my phone rang, it was her. So I acted like nothing was wrong, and I found out she couldn't hear me. I learned about her bad hearing. I felt like such a jerk; I actually thought she was lying to me at first. You know, the typical I know the whole story. I was wrong.

Then I started asking her questions about her birth year, things about us as kids, and favorite Bible verse. I would not have known without asking because we have never talked about verses. We did go to church once in a while as kids. And from time to time, she will tell me about something the church did for her and her husband. I know she said she was saved. She asked Jesus into her heart. She also said she was baptized. I will have to believe that to be true unless she says differently. I believe that God saved her from many things. And in my heart, I know she is saved. I thought that if she were really saved, she would want to talk to me more. That she would try harder after we went to Texas after her last stroke. He gave her another chance. She isn't using it with me. I wonder if out of sight, out of mind is easier for my mother. Being saved doesn't take the memories away of pain you felt or caused. Maybe hearing my voice or seeing my face still brings her a great deal of pain, possibly regret. I have pains, memories, and regret. That's why this is being written.

I know that God will forgive us if we ask. But do we forgive ourselves? I don't always. When will we realize that God sent his son to give us life and save us, not just tell us we are saved to watch us torture ourselves all the days of our lives after receiving salvation! When will I get it completely?

"For God did not send his Son into the world to condemn the world, but to save the world through him" (John 3:17).

Save the world through HIM! We are part of this world, and He wants to save us too! Will you accept that?

So maybe at this time, you don't know about all this God talk or Jesus saving us. I just ask that you keep going. There is so much to learn. The one thing you must know now is that God loves you! If that is hard to grab a hold of, I know. One of my first questions is, why? Even as a child, I thought that was a lie; there is no way God is going to love me. My life is horrible, and He hasn't made it stop. How can He let me be hurt all the time?

It took me a long time to realize God does not cause my hurts and pains. There are evils in this world and evil in people and sin that cause hurts and pains and devastations.

Does God have the ability to stop all of it? Yes, He does. Why doesn't He? I believe it is because He gives us free will. Free will to choose too love and follow him or never grab a hold of his love for us. Free to turn our back and walk away from him. I believe he allows things to happen so we can help guide others through their troubles.

"Praise Be to God and Father of our Lord Jesus Christ, the Father of compassion and the God of all comfort, who comforts us in all our troubles, so that we can comfort those in any trouble with the comfort we ourselves receive from God" (2 Corinthians 1:3–4, NIV).

This is the first piece of Scripture I use when people ask me why God causes hurt. He doesn't cause it but sometimes allows it. If one person goes through a huge pain and turmoil but can reach one other or hundreds with the message of God's love and how they got through it, wouldn't it be worth it? Maybe not right in the moment but after the dust has settled? Even if it's difficult to speak of the pain, would you use it to help others? My answer is yes. That is why you are reading this because I think my pain and choices can help others heal or see God. You are worth it. Even if I don't know your name, or know your face, God does and He says you are worth it!

I believe that God uses the horrible heart-wrenching things in our lives to draw closer to Him. Would we need God as much if this life was perfect? I don't think I would call out to Him even half of what I do. And that sounds arrogant I'm sure. But it is the truth. How often would we need God to help us if our lives were perfect and free from want or pain? None. I believe we would be with Him in heaven at that point.

"Come near to God and he will come near to you" (James 4:8, NIV).

Responses

All scripture is from the NIV bible unless the responder stated another version.

1. LOL.
2. Psalm 139:16 "Your eyes say my unformed body; all the days ordained for me were written in your book before one of them came to be."
3. Philippians 4:13 "I can do all this through him who gives me strength."
   a) There is also a plaque at home that tells about the Proverbs 31:28 woman, that her children will rise up and call her blessed. I don't know that she would say it is her favorite, but I know the verse is true. (She was given the plaque one Mother's Day when she was chosen Mother of the year). That's *my mom!*
4. The Lord's Prayer. Matthew 6:9–13 "Our Father in heaven, hallowed be your name, your kingdom come, your will be done, on earth as it is in heaven. Give us today our daily bread. And forgive us our debts, as we also have forgiven our debtors. And lead us not into temptation but deliver us from the evil one." (4)
5. Romans 8:28 "And we know that in all things God works for the good of those who love him, who have been called according to his purpose." (2)
6. Psalm 23
   a) The Lord is my shepherd, I lack nothing. He makes me lie down in green pastures, he leads me beside quiet waters, he refreshes my soul. He guides me along the right paths for his name's sake. Even though I walk through the darkest valley, I will fear no evil, for you are with me; your rod and your staff, they comfort me. You prepare a table before me in the presence of my enemies. You anoint my head with oil; my cup overflows. Surely your goodness and love will follow me all

the days of my life, and I will dwell in the house of the Lord forever. (7)

7. Psalms.

8. Joshua 24:15 "But if serving the Lord seems undesirable to you, then choose for yourselves this day whom you will serve, whether the gods your ancestors served beyond the Euphrates, or the gods of the Amorites, in whose land you are living. But as for me and my household, we will serve the Lord."

9. Jeremiah 29:11 "For I know the plans I have for you, "declares the Lord, "plans to prosper you and not to harm you, plans to give you hope and a future." (2)

10. Psalm 46:10 "He says, 'Be still, and know that I am God; I will be exalted among the nations, I will be exalted in the earth.'" (2)

11. Psalm 121:1–8 "I lift my eyes to the mountains—where does my help come from? My help comes from the Lord, the maker of heaven and earth. He will not let your foot slip- he who watches over you will not slumber; indeed, he who watches over Israel will neither slumber nor sleep. The Lord watches over you- the Lord are your shade at your right hand; the sun will not harm you by day, nor the moon by night. The Lord will keep you from all harm- he will watch over your life; the Lord will watch over your coming and going both now and forevermore. (2)

12. Psalm 37:4–6 "Take delight in the Lord, and he will give you the desires of your heart. Commit your way to the Lord; trust in him and he will do this: He will make your righteous reward shine like the dawn, your vindication like the noonday sun."

13. Ezra.

14. Philippians 4:6–7 "Do not be anxious about anything, but in every situation, but in every situation, by prayer and petition, with thanksgiving, present your requests to God. And the peace of God, which transcends all understanding, will guard your hearts and your minds in Christ Jesus."

15. John 3:16 "For God so loved the world that he gave his one and only Son, that whoever believes in him shall not perish but have eternal life." (4)

16. Psalm 119:133 "Direct my footsteps according to your word; let no sin rule over me."

17. Matthew 17:20 "He replied, 'Because you have so little faith. Truly I tell you, if you have faith as small as a mustard seed, you can say to this mountain, "Move from here to there," and it will move. Nothing will be impossible for you.'"

18. 1 Corinthians 13:4–8 "Love is patient, love is kind. It does not envy, it does not boast, it is not proud. It does not dishonor others, it is not self-seeking, it is not easily angered, it keeps no record of wrongs. Love does not delight in evil but rejoices with the truth. It always protects, always trusts, always hopes, always perseveres. Love never fails. But where there are prophecies, they will cease; where there are tongues, they will be stilled; where there is knowledge, it will pass away." (2)

19. 1 Peter 5:7 "Cast all your anxiety on him because he cares for you."

20. Matthew 6:33 "But seek first his kingdom and his righteousness, and all these things will be given to you as well."

21. Proverbs 31:10–31: "A wife of noble character who can find? She is worth far more than rubies. Her husband has full confidence in her and lacks nothing of value. She brings him good, not harm, all the days of her life. She selects wool and flax and works with eager hands. She is like the merchant ships, bringing her food from afar. She gets up while it is still night; she provides food for her family and portions for her female servants. She considers a field and buys it; out of her earnings she plants a vineyard. She sets about her work vigorously; her arms are strong for her tasks. She sees that her trading is profitable, and her lamp does not go out at night. In her hands she holds the distaff and grasps the spindle with her fingers. She opens

her arms to the poor and extends her hands to the needy. When it snows, she has no fear for her household; for all of them are clothed in scarlet. She makes coverings for her bed; she is clothed in fine lined and purple. Her husband is respected at the city gate, where he takes his seat among the elders of the land. She makes linen garments and sells them and supplies the merchants with sashes. She is clothed with strength and dignity; she can laugh at the days to come. She speaks with wisdom, and faithful instruction is on her tongue. She watches over the affairs of her household and does not eat the bread of idleness. Her children arise and call her blessed; and her husband also, and he praises her: "Many women do noble things, but you surpass them all." Charm is deceptive, and beauty is fleeting; but a woman who fears the Lord is to be praised. Honor her for all that her hands have done, and let her works bring her praise at the city gate."

22. Luke 17:6 "He replied, 'If you have faith as small as a mustard seed, you can say to this mulberry tree, "Be uprooted and planted in the sea," and it will obey you.'"

23. Proverbs 3:6 "In all your ways submit to him, and he will make your path straight."

24. Proverbs 31:25 "Speak up for those who cannot speak for themselves, for the rights of all who are destitute."

25. None – Mom never read the Bible as far as I know.

26. Psalm 118:24 (NKJV) "This is the day the Lord has made; let us rejoice and be glad in it."

27. Probably John 4. The passage about the woman at the well. The story of that woman and her encounter with Jesus resonates with my mom very much. She even has a tattoo alluding to that passage.

Now it's your turn to answer.

Do you know her favorite bible verse?

_____
_____
_____
_____
_____
_____
_____
_____
_____
_____
_____
_____
_____
_____
_____
_____
_____
_____
_____
_____
_____
_____
_____
_____
_____
_____
_____
_____
_____

Chapter 13

What Is Your Favorite Bible Verse(s)?

I have a few favorite verses and passages. It's trying to figure out what order to place them. A few of them have already been used, but I am going to use them again in this chapter because they are a few of the favorite.

The first one is Proverbs 3:5–6 (NIV): "Trust in the Lord with all your heart and lean not on your own understanding; in all your ways submit to him, and he will make your paths straight."

First, let me say trust is not won easily with me. Not because I am better than anyone else, but past wounds remind me not to get too close. Over and over again, God has proven and shown me that I can trust Him always. I may not like what path He leads me down at first, but I trust that He will protect me and guide me as I go.

I remember the first time our pastor said I should check into becoming a chaplain. I looked at him and laughed. Asking him if he knew me or some of the things I had done. He knew, and he didn't laugh back. I believe God had spoken this to him, and he was being obedient by asking me about checking it out. I fought this idea, even as I researched it. I argued with God about continuing to explore this path out of fear of failure or rejection by others. "God, do you *really know* the things I have done? The things I have said? The places I have been or how I got there? Do you really want me to go to others in need and pray or hold their hand as they breathe their last? You want me to comfort families when my own is messed up on so many levels?"

His response each time I spoke a question was *yes*!

I was and still get terrified some times. Then I remember why I go and who I go for, and I go with confidence even if it is difficult.

> The Lord replied, "My presence will go with you, and I will give you rest." (Exodus 33:14, NIV)

> Then I heard the voice of the Lord saying, "Whom shall I send? And who will go for us?" And I said, "Here am I. Send me!" (Isaiah 6:8, NIV)

> I will instruct you and teach you in the way you should go; I will counsel you with my loving eye on you. (Psalm 32:8, NIV)

So I go. I want to go. Even if that means it is ten minutes or all day. Even if I know it might not end as I want and after I sit in the parking garage at the hospital, crying and sobbing because someone has died. I will still go again. I don't enjoy seeing people hurting in their physical bodies or in their heart. They can't do it alone. I'm not okay with them being in pain alone, without someone supporting them, holding a hand, hugging them, or just being another set of ears as doctors or nurses tell them what is happening or what to expect.

Do I tell others what I do, sometimes I do. I tell my husband who is a great supporter. Once, I called Panda because it was someone she knew. Then there are a few friends that I trust with my emotions that I have called on the way home from an exhausting time at the hospital that will let me vent or cry about what has happened. We all need a sounding board, or we would explode with all the information we hold. Trust me, there are many things I will never tell. Conversations are all confidential. Hospital visits are painful. I do not go to get glory, but someone has to go. Sometimes, God sends others, instead of me. And that is okay too.

One of the passages I identified with the most in the beginning was about the woman at the well. I had lived somewhat like her so often that I felt unworthy of real love, or what I even needed, I did not deserve.

> When a Samaritan woman came to draw water, Jesus said to her, "Will you give me a drink?" (His disciples had gone into the town to buy food.) The Samaritan woman said to him, "You are a Jew and I am a Samaritan woman. How can you ask me for a drink?" (For Jews do not associate with Samaritans.) Jesus answered her, "If you knew the gift of God and who it is that asks you for a drink, you would have asked him and he would have given you living water." "Sir," the woman said, "you have nothing to draw with and the well is deep. Where can you get this living water? Are you greater than our father Jacob, who gave us the well and drank from it himself, as did also his sons and his livestock?" Jesus answered, "Everyone who drinks this water will be thirsty again, but whoever drinks the water I give them will never thirst. Indeed, the water I give them will become in them a spring of water welling up to eternal like." The woman said to him, "Sir, give me this water so that I won't get thirsty and have to keep coming here to draw water." He told her, "Go, call your husband and come back."
>
> "I have no husband," she replied. Jesus said to her, "You are right when you say you have no husband. The fact is, you have had five husbands, and the man you now have is not your husband. What you have just said is quite true." (John 4:7–18)

> Many of the Samaritans from that town believed in him because of the woman's testimony, "He told me everything I ever did." So when the

Samaritans came to him, they urged him to stay with them, and he stayed two days. And because of his words many more became believers. They said to the woman, "We no longer believe just because of what you said; now we have heard for ourselves, and we know that this man really is the Savior of the world." (John 4:39–42)

The tattoo on my back represents these verses. It is a woman with a tear on her cheek, praying with Jesus. The tear to me is a moment when all of the pain and life's failures are washed away. When the choices she made and her sin was washed away and forgiven. A tear of joy for she now knows what it looks like and feels like to have the love she so desperately had been looking for right in front of her, and it is peace.

"The Lord will fight for you; you need only to be still" (Exodus 14:14, NIV).

There have many battles that if I would have not been still, not stopped to pray first or often, had I reacted with my emotions first, the situation would have been a lot worse than when it started!

Moments when a child acted a fool and caused pain and turmoil within the family, had I acted first and not given it to God, I would have been in trouble. Words would have been said that might not have ever been repaired. There were moments in my marriage when I did the wrong thing. I did not always let God guide me when dealing with my mother either. I am learning how to do that.

That brings me to the next favorite.

For the spirit God gave us does not make us timid, but gives us power, love, and self-discipline. (2 Timothy 1:7, NIV)

For God did not give us a Spirit of fear but of power and love and self-control. (2 Timothy 1:7, NET)

> For God has not given us a spirit of fear and timidity, but of power, love, and self-discipline. (2 Timothy 1:7, NLT)

I really like all three versions of this verse! We are not meant to be doormats for people to walk all over. We shouldn't be afraid of things in life all of the time either. We are to love, have compassion, have self-control over our behavior. Basically, I see it as I need to act like an adult and not a child on the playground who can't get along with others. I am not always like that. I have found it takes a great amount of strength and prayer to walk away from some situations instead of speaking what I am feeling. Have I failed at this before? Oh my, yes. I will say, the other day I did very well and left a situation before I blew it! Yes, I was and am very proud of myself over this one!

I am a child of God, as well as a mother and grandmother. Sometimes I have the claws out before the prayer on my lips. But not this time! And for those that have had that self-control, woo-hoo! Celebrate it!

> Love is patient, love is kind. It does not envy, it does not boast, it is not proud. It does not dishonor others, it is not self-seeking, it is not easily angered, it keeps no record of wrongs. Love does not delight in evil but rejoices with the truth. It always protects, always trusts, always hopes, always, perseveres. (1 Corinthians 13:4–7, NIV)

> Love is patient and kind. Love is not jealous or boastful or proud or rude. It does not demand its own way. It is not irritable, and it keeps no record of being wronged. It does not rejoice about injustice but rejoices whenever the truth wins out. Love never gives up, never loses faith, is always hopeful, and endures through every circumstance. (1 Corinthians 13:4–7, NLT)

Those passages speak for themselves.

The next passage holds a special place in my heart. There was a dear, sweet lady who ended up in the hospital with a broken leg. The doctors found out she had so many more health problems that she never went home. They ended up moving her after a few surgeries to a nursing home type facility. There were times I visited almost every day for a few weeks and then once a month. It tore me up to see her in pain and slipping away from her family and her friends and I. We did become better friends when she was there, over a year, I think. I would sneak her vanilla pudding once in a while; it was not sugar-free. She would sometimes forget my name, but if someone said pudding, she knew instantly who I was. I miss her. I cried when she struggled to breathe or remember who people were. But if I asked where does your help come from? Every answer was, "from the Lord!" Every single time, she would say that. Oh, how she loved the Lord! I know she is in heaven, feeling no pain, but I can't help be a little sad I won't see her face on Sundays at church or passing in the store. I loved her heart and her smile and her laugh, her love for pudding, and the childlike way she would smirk knowing it was a treat, and she enjoyed it. I know that she would look at me right now if she were here and tell me, "Your help comes from the Lord, Christy, seek Him in this moment!"

I miss her.

> I lift up my eyes to the mountains—
> Where does my help come from?
> My help comes from the Lord,
> the Maker of heaven and earth.
> He will not let your foot slip—
> he who watches over you will not slumber;
> indeed, he who watches over Israel
> will neither slumber nor sleep.
> The Lord watches over you—
> the Lord is your shade at your
> right hand;
> the sun will not harm you by day,

> nor the moon by night.
> The Lord will keep you from all harm—
> he will watch over your life;
> the Lord will watch over your coming and going
> both now and forevermore. (Psalm 121:1–8,
> NIV)

Well, I didn't hit save before I stepped away for a moment, and the computer restarted with updates! The only loss was a nice-size paragraph, and yes, I am tearing up a bit. I know it's only small amount of writing but . . .

I get upset about losing a small section of work, and it doesn't compare to the last piece of scripture I had added.

"Jesus wept" (John 11:35).

He was weeping because he saw how sad Martha was at the loss of her brother, Lazarus. Even though he told her Lazarus would rise again. He felt that pain, the pain his friends had for the loss of their brother.

Someone I cared for died, and we knew she was going to. It wasn't a surprise at all. I asked someone why I couldn't stop crying even though I knew she was with Jesus. He said that even Jesus cried for his friends. So I allowed myself to weep for a moment or two more.

> When Mary reached the place where Jesus was
> and saw him, she fell at his feet and said, "Lord,
> if you had been here, my brother would not have
> died." When Jesus saw her weeping, and the
> Jews had come along with her also weeping, he
> was deeply moved in spirit and troubled. (John
> 11:32–33, NIV)

So, think about this for a moment.

Jesus *knew* that Lazarus was going to rise again! He knew this, yet he still wept for the pain that his friend felt!

Jesus cared and was *deeply* moved in spirit and troubled when he saw others weeping. Can you wrap your head around how much love He had for them, mourning a man that would rise again and live again, that it moved him that much to tears. Not just tears, but he wept!

How much love do He and His Father have for us, that Jesus would give his life for us? How much love must He feel for not just one but all of the human race to go through what He did, the beatings, being spat at, cursed, accused, and the torment, being hung on a cross by nails in his feet and hands, his side pierced, death, a time, however, brief, separated from the Father for the purpose of taking all of our sin. He did that for us! He endured that pain for you and me! Those nails did not hold Him on that cross or prevent Him from getting down. He was the Son of God; He could have said no, I'm not doing this for a people that will turn their backs on You, Father! That will deny You and walk away!

But He didn't get down!

> About three in the afternoon Jesus cried out in a loud voice, "Eli, Eli, lema sabachthani?" (which means "My God, My God, why have you forsaken me?"). (Matthew 27:46, NIV)

> It was now about noon, and darkness came over the whole land until three in the afternoon, for the sun stopped shining. And the curtain of the temple was torn in two. Jesus called out with a loud voice, "Father, into your hands I commit my spirit." When he had said this, he breathed his last. (Luke 23:44–46, NIV)

> At noon, darkness came over the whole land until three in the afternoon and at three in the afternoon Jesus cried out in a loud voice, "Eloi, Eloi, lema sabachthani?" (Which means "My God, my God, why have you forsaken me?").

When some of those standing near heard this, they said, "Listen, he's calling Elijah." Someone ran, filled a sponge with wine vinegar, put it on a staff, and offered it to Jesus to drink. "Now leave him alone. Let's see if Elijah comes to take him down," he said.

With a loud cry, Jesus breathed his last. The curtain of the temple was torn in two from top to bottom. And when the centurion, who stood there in front of Jesus, saw how he died, he said, "Surely this man was the Son of God!" (Mark 15:33–39, NIV)

Later, knowing that everything had now been finished, and so that Scripture would be fulfilled, Jesus said, "I am thirsty." A jar of wine vinegar was there, so they soaked a sponge in it, put the sponge on a stalk of the hyssop plant, and lifted it to Jesus' lips. When he had received the drink, Jesus said, "It is finished." With that, he bowed his head and gave up his spirit. (John 19:28–30, NIV)

How much does God love you that He was willing to give His only son to suffer for us?

If Jesus would weep for his friends and go through all of that for us, do you think He loves you? That His Father loves you?

I am thankful for that love, a love that I do not deserve and that I cannot earn.

Responses

1. Romans 8:9 "You, however, are not in the realm of the flesh but are in the realm of the Spirit, if indeed the Spirit of God lives in you. And if anyone does not have the Spirit of Christ, they do not belong to Christ."

2. Philippians 4:13 "I can do all this through him who gives me strength." (15)

3. 2 Corinthians 1:3–4 "Praise be to the God and Father of our Lord Jesus Christ, the Father of compassion and the God of all comfort, who comforts us un all our troubles, so that we can comfort those in any trouble with the comfort we ourselves receive from God."

4. Psalm 139:14 "I praise you because I am fearfully and wonderfully made; your works are wonderful, I know that full well."

5. 1 Corinthians 13:4–7 "Love is patient, love is kind. It does not envy, it does not boast, it is not proud. It does not dishonor others, it is not self-seeking, it is not easily angered, it keeps no record of wrongs. Love does not delight in evil but rejoices with the truth. It always protects, always trusts, always hopes, always perseveres."

6. Matthew 6:9–13 "Our Father in heaven, hallowed be your name, your kingdom come, your will be done, on earth as it is in heaven. Give us today our daily bread. And forgive us our debts, as we also have forgiven our debtors. And lead us not into temptation, but deliver us from the evil one." (3)

7. Hosea 2:19 "I will betroth you to me forever; I will betroth you in righteousness and justice, in love and compassion."

8. Proverbs 3:5–6 "Trust in the Lord with all your heart and lean not on your own understanding; in all your ways submit to him, and he will make your paths straight." (4)

9. John 3:16 "For God so loved the world that he gave his one and only Son, that whoever believes in him shall not perish but have eternal life." (10)

10. Psalms.
11. Jeremiah 29:11 "'For I know the plans I have for you,' declares the Lord, 'plans to prosper you and not to harm you, plans to give you hope and a future.'" (3)
12. Psalm 23:1–6
    The Lord is my shepherd, I lack nothing. He makes me lie down in green pastures, he leads me beside quiet waters, he refreshes my soul. He guides me along the right paths for his name's sake. Even though I walk through the darkest valley, I will fear no evil, for you are with me; your rod and your staff, they comfort me. You prepare a table before me in the presence of my enemies. You anoint my head with oil; my cup overflows. Surely your goodness and love will follow me all the days of my life, and I will dwell in the house of the Lord forever. (2)
13. Philippians 2:9–11 "Therefore God exalted him to the highest place and gave him the name that is above every name, that at the name of Jesus every knee should bow, in heaven and on earth and under the earth, and every tongue acknowledge that Jesus Christ is Lord, to the glory of God the Father."
14. Psalm 26:10 "In whose hands are wicked schemes, whose right hands are full of bribes."
15. Psalm 127:3–5 "Children are a heritage from the Lord, offspring a reward from him. Like arrows in the hands of a warrior are children born in one's youth. Blessed is the man whose quiver is full of them. They will not be put to shame when they contend with their opponents in court."
16. Matthew 28:20 "And teaching them to obey everything I have commanded you. And surely I am with you always, to the very end of the age."
17. 1 Corinthians 13
    If I speak in the tongues of men or of angels, but do not have love, I am only a resounding gong or a clanging cymbal. If I have the gift of prophecy and can fathom all mysteries and all knowledge, and if I have a faith that can move

mountains, but do not have love, I am nothing. If I give all I possess to the poor and give over my body to hardship that I may boast, but do not have love, I gain nothing. Love is patient, love is kind. It does not envy, it does not boast, it is not proud. It does not dishonor others, it is not self-seeking, it is not easily angered, it keeps no record of wrongs. Love does not delight in evil but rejoices with the truth. It always protects, always trusts, always hopes, always perseveres. Love never fails. But where there are prophecies, they will cease; where there are tongues, they will be stilled' where there is knowledge, it will pass away. For we know in part and we prophesy in part, but when completeness comes, what is in part disappears. When I was a child I talked like a child, I thought like a child, I reasoned like a child. When I became a man, I put the ways of childhood behind me. For now we see only a reflection as in a mirror; then we shall see face to face. Now I know in part; then I shall know fully, even as I am fully known. And now these three remain: faith, hope and love. But the greatest of these is love. (2)

18. Ecclesiastes 3:1–8

There is a time for everything, and a season for every activity under the heavens:

a time to be born and a time to die,
a time to plant and a time to uproot,
a time to kill and a time to heal,
a time to tear down and a time to build,
a time to weep and a time to laugh,
a time to mourn and a time to dance,
a time to scatter stones and a time to gather them,
a time to embrace and a time to refrain from embracing,
a time to search and a time to give up,
a time to keep and a time to throw away,
a time to tear and a time to mend,
a time to be silent and a time to speak,
a time to love and a time to hate,

a time for war and a time for peace.

19. Isaiah 41:13 "For I am the Lord your God who takes hold of your right hand and says to you, Do not fear; I will help you."

20. John 15:4 "Remain in me, as I also remain in you. No branch can bear fruit by itself; it must remain in the vine. Neither can you bear fruit unless you remain in me."

21. Proverbs 31:30 "Charm is deceptive, and beauty is fleeting; but a woman who fears the Lord is to be praised."

22. Psalm 46:10 "He says, 'Be still, and know that I am God; I will be exalted among the nations, I will be exalted in the earth.'" (2)

23. Proverbs 31:10–31 (2)

A wife of noble character who can find? She is worth far more than rubies. Her husband has full confidence in her and lacks nothing of value. She brings him good, not harm, all the days of her life. She selects wool and flax and works with eager hands. She is like the merchant ships, bringing her food from afar. She gets up while it is still night; she provides food for her family and portions for her female servants. She considers a field and buys it; out of her earnings she plants a vineyard. She sets about her work vigorously; her arms are strong for her tasks. She sees that her trading is profitable, and her lamp does not go out at night. In her hands she holds the distaff and grasps the spindle with her fingers. She opens her arms to the poor and extends her hands to the needy. When it snows, she has no fear for her household; for all of them are clothed in scarlet. She makes coverings for her bed; she is clothed in fine lined and purple. Her husband is respected at the city gate, where he takes his seat among the elders of the land. She makes linen garments and sells them, and supplies the merchants with sashes. She is clothed with strength and dignity; she can laugh at the days to come. She speaks with wisdom, and faithful instruction is on her tongue. She watches over the affairs of her household and does not eat the bread of idleness. Her children arise and call her blessed; and her husband also, and he praises her: "Many women do noble things, but you surpass them all." Charm is deceptive, and beauty is fleeting; but a woman who fears the Lord is to be praised. Honor her for all that her hands have done, and let her works bring her praise at the city gate.

24. Ephesians 1:3 "Praise be to the God and Father of our Lord Jesus Christ, who has blessed us in the heavenly realms with every spiritual blessing in Christ."

25. Ephesians 1:4–5 "For he chose us in him before the creation of the world to be holy and blameless in his sight. In love he predestined us for adoption to sonship through Jesus Christ, in accordance with his pleasure and will."

26. Exodus 14:14 "The Lord will fight for you; you need only to be still." (3)

27. Isaiah 53:5 "But he was pierced for our transgressions, he was crushed for our iniquities; the punishment that brought us peace was on him, and by his wounds we are healed."

28. John 14:2–5 "My Father's house has many rooms; if that were not so, would I have told you that I am going there to prepare a place for you? And if go and prepare a place for you, I will come back and take you to be with me that you also may be where I am. You know the way to the place where I am going." Thomas said to him, "Lord, we don't know where you are going, so how can we know the way?"

29. Matthew 7:12 "So in everything, do to others what you would have them do to you, for this sums up the Law and the Prophets."

30. Matthew 6:34 "Therefore do not worry about tomorrow, for tomorrow will worry about itself. Each day has enough trouble of its own."

31. Psalm 121
I lift up my eyes to the mountains—
where does my help come from?
My help comes from the Lord, the Maker of heaven and earth.

He will not let your foot slip—
he who watches over you will not slumber;
indeed, he who watches over Israel will neither slumber
nor sleep.
The Lord watches over you—
the Lord is your shade at you right hand;
the sun will not harm you by day,
nor the moon by night.
The Lord will keep you from all harm—
he will watch over your life;
the Lord will watch over your coming
and going
both now and forevermore.

32. 1 Corinthians 6:19–20 "Do you not know that your bodies are temples of the Holy Spirit, who is in you, whom you have received from God? You are not your own; you were bought at a price. Therefore, honor God with your bodies."

33. Romans 8:28 "And we know that in all things God works for the good of those who love him, who have been called according to his purpose."

34. Matthew 16:26 "What good will it be for someone to gain the whole world, yet forfeit their soul? Or what can anyone give in exchange for their soul?"

35. Isaiah 41:10 "So do not fear, for I am with you; do not be dismayed, for I am your God. I will strengthen you and help you; I will uphold you with my righteous right hand."

36. Genesis 50:20 "You intended to harm me, but God intended it for good to accomplish what is now being done, the saving of many lives."

37. Romans 8:37–39
No, in all these things we are more than conquerors through him who loved us. For I am convinced that neither death nor life, neither angels nor demons, neither the present nor depth, nor anything else in all creation, will be able to separate us from the love of God that is in Christ Jesus our Lord.

38. Matthew 5:3–11

Blessed are the poor in spirit,
for theirs is the kingdom of heaven.
Blessed are those who mourn,
for they will be comforted.
Blessed are the meek,
for they will inherit the earth.
Blessed are those who hunger and thirst for righteousness,
for they will be filled.
Blessed are the merciful, for they will be shown mercy.
Blessed are the pure in heart, for they will see God.
Blessed are the peacemakers,
for they will be called children of God.
Blessed are those who are persecuted because of righteousness, for theirs is the kingdom of heaven.
Blessed are you when people insult you, persecute you and falsely say all kinds of evil against you because of me. Rejoice and be glad, because great is your reward in heaven, for in the same way they persecuted the prophets who were before you.

39. Psalm 91

Whoever dwells in the shelter of the Most High will rest in the shadow of the Almighty. I will say of the Lord, "He is my refuge and my fortress, my God, in whom I trust." Surely he will save you from the fowler's snare and from the deadly pestilence. He will cover you with his feathers, and under his wings you will find refuge; his faithfulness will be your shield and rampart. You will not fear the terror of night, nor the arrow that flies by day, nor the pestilence that stalks in the darkness, nor the plague that destroys at midday. A thousand may fall at your side, ten thousand at your right hand, but it will not come near you. You will only observe with your eyes and see the punishment of the wicked. If you say, "The Lord is my refuge," and you make the Most High your dwelling, no harm will overtake you, no disaster will come near your tent. For he will command his angels concerning you to guard you in all your ways; they will lift you up in their hands, so that you will not strike your foot against a stone. You will tread on the lion and the cobra; you will trample the great lion and the serpent. "Because he loves me," says the Lord, "I will rescue him; I will protect him, for he acknowledges my name. He will call on me, and I will answer him; I will be with him in trouble, I will deliver him and honor him. With long life I will satisfy him and show him my salvation."

40. 1 John 1:5 "This is the message we have heard from him and declare to you: God is light; in him there is no darkness at all."

41. Matthew 7:12 "So in everything, do to others what you would have them do to you, for this sums up the Law and the Prophets."

42. Philippians 2:1–5
Therefore, if you have any encouragement from being united with Christ, if any comfort form his love, if any common sharing in the Spirit, if any tenderness and compassion, then make my joy complete by being like- minded, having the same love, being one in spirit and of one mind. Do nothing out of selfish ambition or vain conceit. Rather, in humility value others about yourselves, not looking to your own interests but each of you to the interests of the others. In your relationships with one another, have the same mindset as Christ Jesus:

43. Psalm 28:7 "The Lord is my strength and my shield; my heart trusts in him, and he helps me. My heart leaps for joy, and with my song I praise him."

44. Galatians 2:20 "I have been crucified with Christ and I no longer live, but Christ lives in me. The life I now live in the body, I live by faith in the Son of God, who loved me and gave himself for me."

45. Ezekiel has been very impactful to me, as well as the book of Hosea, which is a much more recent discovery.
Ezekiel 37:1–14

The hand of the Lord was on me, and he brought me out by the Spirit of the Lord and set me in the middle of a valley; it was full of bones. He led me back and forth among them, and I saw a great many bones on the floor of the valley, bones that were very dry. He asked me, "Son of man, can these bones live?" I said, "Sovereign Lord, you alone know." Then he said to me, "Prophesy to these bones and say to them, 'Dry bones, hear the word of the Lord! This is what the Sovereign Lord says to these bones: I will make breath enter you, and you will come to life. I will attach tendons to you and make flesh come upon you and cover you with skin; I will put breath in you, and you will come to life. Then you will know that I am the Lord.'" So I prophesied as I was commanded. And as I was prophesying, there was a noise, a rattling sound, and the bones came together, bone to bone. I looked, and tendons and flesh appeared on them and skin covered them, but there was no breathe in them. Then he said to me, "Prophesy to the breath; prophesy, son of man, and say to it, 'This is what the Sovereign Lord says: Come, breath, from the four winds and breathe into these slain, that they may live.'" So I prophesied as he commanded me, and breath entered them; they came to life and stood up on their feet—a vast army. Then he said to me: "Son of man, these bones are the people of Israel. They say, 'Our bones are dried up and our hope is gone; we are cut off.' Therefore prophesy and say to them: 'This is what the Sovereign Lord says: My people, I am going to open your graves and bring you up from them; I will bring you back to the land of Israel. Then you, my people, will know that I am the Lord, when I open your graves and bring you up from them. I will put my Spirit in you and you will live, and I will settle you in your own land. The you will know that I the Lord have spoken, and I have done it, declares the Lord.'"

Now it's your turn to answer.

What is your favorite bible verse(s)?

_____
_____
_____
_____
_____
_____
_____
_____
_____
_____
_____
_____
_____
_____
_____
_____
_____
_____
_____
_____
_____
_____
_____
_____
_____
_____
_____
_____
_____

Chapter 14

A Moment She Showed Wrath and Should Have Shown Mercy

"My dear brothers and sisters, take note of this; Everyone should be quick to listen, slow to speak and slow to become angry, because human anger does not produce the righteousness that God desires" (James 1:19–20, NIV).

As I sit here, thinking about moments my mother, in my opinion, should have shown mercy instead of anger; it reminds me of all the times I did this when my kids were younger. I know parents get mad, and often, that anger comes out first. I would like to think I spoke the word *sorry* often but not as often as I should have. I don't hesitate to apologize now, but my wrath does not come quickly now.

I know when we made my father mad, she would snap at us instead of being angry with him for being a jerk to everyone. Obviously, none of us wanted to experience his bad inexcusable moods. Blaming your children for your husband's temper, that is just plain stupid.

There was one time when we were younger, my sister and I were chasing each other through the house. I was chasing her, and I tried to get into the bedroom. My big toe got caught in the door, and it was bleeding. Of course, I am going to cry, it hurt. My mother freaked out so bad on her. I was trying to tell her it was my fault too, and I was okay. She grabbed my sister by the arms and was screaming in her face shaking her. I cried more about that than my toe. It was like she snapped into someone I didn't know. You know why she was so mad? Because if someone let it slip to my father what happened, he would be mad at her for not controlling the kids! I felt horrible for my sister. I was so angry at my mother that I don't think I talked to her the rest of the day. My sis and I fought or teased a lot. And sometimes, she was a little meaner, but she did not deserve that treatment that day or ever. It was like some monster had snagged my sister. And she looked so afraid, so afraid I could feel the fear roll off her and fill the room. I was afraid for her.

One of the other times my mother showed wrath when she should have hugged me and said she loved me was when she found out that my father molested me for years. She was so mad at me. After my sis ran away and then I was taken out of the house, the county set up supervised visits with us, my brothers and our mother. We didn't talk about why this was the only way to see each other. We talked about stupid stuff like the dogs chewed my holly hobby doll she made me. She would bring a few of our things each visit, but it was stuff that didn't fit, nothing we asked for. The visits were once a week for about two, maybe three months. Then it would be two weeks between visits with less interaction, or obvious she wasn't interested in being there like she had a better place to be. Then it moved to once a month with no connection.

I can still picture the CYS office and her not looking back when she left us. When the visits went to once a month, we didn't see our brothers. The oldest sister we never saw. Not until court. What a shamble that was. All I will say about court is my mother would glare at me and shake her head. I was actually told to say I lied so I could come home and they would love me again. Again? So you stopped loving me because I told the truth? You stopped loving me because I made you both look like what you were, bad parents, and monsters? I would have rather had wrath than rejection. Now it's the other way around.

When I think of all the times I ran away from the foster homes and went back to them, just to earn their love, it makes me sick. When a child feels they have to work that hard for the positive attention and love, it means they never had it anyway!

Love is patient, love is kind. It does not envy, it
does not boast, it is not proud. It does not dis-

honor other's, it is not self-seeking. It is not easily angered, it keeps no record of wrongs. Love does not delight in evil but rejoices with the truth. It always protects, always trusts, always hopes, always perseveres. Love never fails. (1 Corinthians 13:4–8, NIV)

A gentle answer turns away wrath, but a harsh word stirs up anger. The tongue of the wise adorns knowledge, but the mouth of the fool gushes folly. (Proverbs 15:1–2, NIV)

A hot-tempered person stirs up conflict, but the one who is patient calms a quarrel. (Proverbs 15:18, NIV)

Responses

1. Addiction.
2. When I accidentally knocked my little sisters tooth out when pulling her on a sled.
3. Well, I believed I deserved all the wrath I got, but she now says she was too hard on me as a child. I would probably have agreed then, but I am grateful for it now.
4. When my sister would take my things without asking.
5. When my marriage fell apart.
6. When I wrecked my car and was injured as an adult.
7. I needed help escaping an abusive relationship.
8. When I would test my independence growing up.
9. Most always.
10. Always.
11. When we needed a swat, we got a swat.
12. When my brother got me in trouble.
13. My mother was a figure of mercy.
14. Never.
15. When I was busy doing things for my kids, and she forgot I wouldn't be at an event.
16. When I smarted off one time, she lost her cool.
17. She was not really the disciplinarian, so she showed mercy a lot.
18. When I went to a boyfriend's, and she forgot I woke her and asked to go.
19. When I didn't dust all the furniture.
20. When I made little mistakes.
21. Not often enough.
22. LOL, when I fell into a ditch with my new Easter coat on, age five or six.
23. I tried to explain the difference between Christians and Catholics.
24. When she accused me of doing drugs and getting high because my friends and I liked the smell of a certain

cologne. I've never done drugs my entire life, and she was certain I was.

25. When I got pregnant with my first child.(2)
26. When her husband molested me.
27. Bad mother.
28. Every time she broke up with a boyfriend, it was my fault.
29. She broke three of my ribs and gave me a concussion for failing a class.
30. When I came to her about how I was truly feeling.
31. When I was involved in a car accident ten years ago.
32. *Always!*
33. This is touchy. Very touchy . . . her and her sister ganged up on me when I had to go to court about being date raped. I think it was just hard for everyone to wrap their heads around that I could hold so much in for so long. I myself was not mentally stable for a long time, but that's all in the past. And when it counted, she was by my side and watched me crumble for years and helped me be strong even if it meant breaking her down. I will never forget that.
34. When I told her I'd been hurt by someone.
35. When my current husband abuses me, she blocks me instead of being there for me as a support system.
36. Most times.
37. Too many to pick only one.
38. Most times wrath came out, I deserved it.
39. When my future mother-in-law gave her money to cover part of my wedding venue.
40. When I misunderstood an arrangement we made this summer.
41. When I had an ATV accident at work.
42. When relationships are brought up or talk of dating.
43. When I found out at eighteen I was pregnant with my first.
44. When I was head over heels in love with a guy at age fourteen (at least I thought I was), she would have gotten further with me by being merciful.
45. Too many to recall one.

46. Boyfriends—her explaining the traits she recognized would have kept me from making several mistakes.
47. Very patient with me.
48. When my other siblings did wrong and the blame was placed on me as the oldest.
49. My mother was very volatile and didn't often show mercy.
50. When I told her I was being sexually molested.
51. No, Mom loved unconditionally.
52. When I needed to talk to her about anything when I was growing up.
53. More times than I'd like to think. We have always had a rocky relationship when it came to my choices.
54. Maybe when I was sixteen to eighteen years old, but understandably because it was my life to live. Found out it is truly not my own!
55. Every time she got the apple tree switch swinging "*ouch.*"
56. When I would fight with my sister. One time she thought I said something that I didn't, and she got really angry.
57. Toward my dad with visitation and child support.
58. Never.
59. It was all the time with her.
60. My mom used to be a pretty angry person, so there are probably a few. One instance, I remember was when I was younger. My sister had chosen to move out and in with her boyfriend, right out of high school on unpleasant terms. She had a history of choosing guys over her family, and this was another slap in the face to my mom, which I understand. My mom was so angry she flipped the kitchen table. We joke about it now, but back then, it scared me.

Now it's your turn to answer.

A moment she showed wrath and should have shown mercy?

_____
_____
_____
_____
_____
_____
_____
_____
_____
_____
_____
_____
_____
_____
_____
_____
_____
_____
_____
_____
_____
_____
_____
_____
_____
_____
_____

Chapter 15

Is There a Time When You Showed Your Mother Wrath Instead of Mercy?

Yes, there is. I never really showed her disrespect growing up. You just didn't, or there would be heck to pay. That threat of when your father gets home, no one wanted him to come home anyway. And not come home and "deal" with us. I never yelled at her; I don't even think I ever told her no. I did scare her with a snake once. All of us kids worked in a strawberry field behind the house, and on the lunch break, I caught a snake and took it to the house. The door was locked, so I knocked on it and that woke up my mom. Being half asleep and a snake in your face, I got yelled at. I laughed, and she yelled more. And as I walked away, I was grumbling after she shut the door. That's really the most disrespect I think I showed when I was younger.

It was another story all together with each foster home I was in from seven to fifteen. I was in and out of the foster care system when I was younger, removed multiple times because my father's discipline was actually abuse and beatings. I was finally removed at twelve for good. The group home (my third placement after being removed) mother I couldn't stand. She was so distant, except to her kids. And of course, they could do no wrong. We would all sneak out at night with the boy's group-home. Her daughter would say she was just trying to get us to come back. She got in some trouble but not like the rest of the "foster or group home kids." I was so bitter and angry. I didn't ask to be there, with another family, other girls from other broken and destroyed homes. I did everything I could to make them mad, everything.

I got braces when I was thirteen to fourteen, and they took half my weekly allowance because I use to sneak out and run away all the time, and they thought it would stop me from doing those things and it did not. I would get seven dollars a week instead of fourteen dollars. So every Saturday morning, I would walk two to three miles to the local drug store and buy new makeup if I needed it, a soda, and gum. Then to dairy queen for a small blizzard and a final stop at the gas station for a pack of Marlboro's at $ .72 to $ .78 a pack. That covered the whole seven dollars for the week.

Since my mouth was so sensitive to the pain of getting braces on and the tightening every month, they gave me Tylenol 3 codeine tablets to take half-an hour before my orthodontist appointments. The problem with that was the foster parent let me keep them in my possession. So I quit taking a half tablet and took a whole. Go back to school after the appointment and lay down in the nurse's room until fifteen minutes before school was out when they woke me up. Once a month, I would do that. And if I was having a crappy day, I would take one part way through the day and go sleep.

Life was a struggle then, we were going through court hearings, and I was not handling it well, actually not at all. Counseling was not cutting it. I snuck boys in my room a lot more, ran away, I would sneak out at least once or twice a week. The cops were called every time a boy was found in the house, or I just didn't come home. It got to the point when I would sneak out, and I was too tired to walk back to the group home, or whoever I was with wouldn't drop me off close to the house then I stopped at the police station. The first time I did that the officers couldn't believe it. They knew who I lived with and would try and talk me out of behaving like this, give me something to eat and take me back to the house. They always warned me about hooking up with the wrong guys. And how I was so young and on and on. The same things I have told my foster girls.

My group home parents put an alarm on my door. I had thirty seconds before it sounded. When they found out I was still getting out but through the bedroom window they, put a lock on the window. The first one was so easy to pick, so I came and went through the window. After a while, they realized I was still getting out, so they replaced it with a heavy-duty lock I couldn't pick. So I cut it. Once again, I was able to get out.

The more attention I got from the older guys, the more things I did. I was smoking pot, smoking cigarettes, taking speed, being sexually active. We broke into an empty house that was for sale and partied in it and trashed the place. I went to a detention center instead of back to the group home because I thought I was so tough and said I'm not going back. I was there for a few days and realized I was not that tough. I was scared of the doors slamming shut before another opened; I felt so trapped. After the weekend was over, they called my caseworker and let me go. I ended up getting a STD because of that whole outing at thirteen to fourteen. What the heck was I doing? I realized that I just didn't care. Why should I? I ran away so many times and ended up going twenty to thirty minutes back to my parents' house.

One of the rides I got was from a neighbor of my parents'. He was in my area because he had family in the next development. He had his infant kid in the truck with him in the car seat, so I had to sit next to him. He was hitting the cocaine pretty hard. He ended up giving me a ride, but while doing so, he was snorting and had me steer the truck. When I was done steering, he forced my hand onto his penis that was out. Every time I pulled away, he pulled me back to him. Another adult who figured I was free for the taking. He actually told me he would tell my father I was being disrespectful if I didn't do as he said. Even though I was trying to go back home after all they had done, disrespecting an adult is something you just didn't do. He tried to get me to go into his house first, but I told him I would be back later (again, you don't disrespect an adult), but I had to see my parents first. I was afraid he would come get me and offer to take me back to the foster home. He was a friend of my parents, they did drugs together, we did laundry at their house, and when he worked for a chip company, he would bring the out-of-date cakes and chips to our house for us kids. As a kid, I trusted him. I think about it now, and anyone of my parents' friends that stuck around through the abuse charges and in and out of foster homes, I should have known they were no good.

I don't think I ever said anything to my father about it. In my father's eyes, it was okay for him to molest me but no one else. So my father would have hurt him. I know how sick that sounds. And as I tell you these things, I feel as if I must apologize for the way I grew up. As if it is my fault and you will turn your head and look away in disgust if we were to ever meet.

Why did I just say all of this? Why did I share all of that? Because even after all that, my mother did not do or not protect me from, I loved her as a child. And I needed to lash out at someone. It couldn't be her. I felt guilty for wanting a good mom. Guilty for wanting a woman, a mom to teach me, show me what I needed to know without being hurt. To have someone to talk to and hug me when I had a bad dream or was afraid or just to say they loved me. And I didn't want her to think I was betraying her. That I was okay in the foster or group homes, that I was happy to feel safe, to know what safe looked like and felt like. I couldn't turn my back on her the way she did me. So I made it hell, at least, it wouldn't be a lie.

I was always being hateful to my other mothers. Even when we went to court the last time for the child abuse/molestation case, I couldn't be mean to her for not loving me. I just kept looking at her saying I was sorry. I couldn't finish testifying against my father; he sat in the court room smiling at me. My mother and grandmother stood outside the door looking in, staring at me. I was thirteen to fourteen. I wanted to put him away in jail. He would have gone for a long time. If I could testify, there were ten others that would follow me. I wanted to do it, even after the break we took, but they told me I couldn't handle it. And since I was abused the very morning of the day I was taken away, I had to testify first.

I let everyone down. I let my sister down that ran away and saved me from the situation. I let me down my brothers and the abuse increased and got even worse so they had to be removed from the house. When the boys were taken, no kids meant she got it all, and I ran again.

I was horrible to the foster mothers in my life. I believe now that they really wanted to care for me, to give me what I needed. I didn't know how to accept that. It was so foreign to me. I was afraid.

Even after I was married the first time and separated, my last foster mom tried to help me. Even after many, many hurtful words were traded back and forth over the years. I treated her like crap. She wanted to adopt me when I was fifteen, but to me, it was a betrayal of my real mom. I was afraid my real mom would be hurt if I chose another mom to love me, even after her proving time and time again I was not important to her. Even though, the parental rights were terminated sometime after the court hearing fiasco.

I was a horrible teenager. We moved to West Virginia; I ran away around the time I turned sixteen. Quit school, got pregnant, never went back. I hurt her and my foster dad, the two girls they had. I just didn't care anymore. No one had the right to tell me how to live or what to do if they were not going to stick around and prove I was worth it. So why not sabotage all that they tried to do? I was tired of people telling me how to feel or what to feel. Don't date him, or him or him, your grades are bad, stop skipping school. See, I was a horrible teenager. I thought somehow it was okay to be fifteen and date a twenty-eight-year-old. How dare they not want this for me? I wanted out. So obviously there would be hurts.

They moved back to Oregon, I stayed in West Virginia. I felt stuck again. I felt they proved me right; they couldn't handle me and they didn't want me, they didn't fight for me. Deep down, I wanted her to come to get me, to look at me, and say, "Christy, you are a pain but we love you and want you!" I would have gone back. The only message I was sending because they did not speak my teenage language was you don't want to be here, and we want you happy so we won't force you to stay.

Even after that, years later after hateful words spoken by both and a time of complete isolation from them because of the active alcohol and drug addiction, we connected again. She knew I had cleaned up and was doing better. And the man I was with (my husband now) was going through a divorce, couldn't spend quality time with his kids with me around. I don't blame his ex for that; I wouldn't want my kids around a woman who I knew was a drug addict or alcoholic who had been clean less than a year.

In a few ways, I envied the type of mother that she is. No one can ever look at her or behind her back and say she was a bad mom ever. And to be honest, if they did that person would need to have a chat with me. I have a lot of respect for her. We talked, and he and I decided it was time to let go of each other for his kid's sake. So my daughter and I went to spend time with the foster mom and the family for a while. Actually, the plan was to move back to Oregon for good. I was going to get myself set up, I took a computer class, planned on getting a job, and stay in Oregon. I missed the love of my life in Pennsylvania. And my daughter missed the man she called Daddy. He wasn't doing well with the situation either. Yes, he got to spend more time with the kids, but he missed us too. We decided it would only be for the remainder of the summer. I upset the foster mom, again.

I moved in with my real grandparents. Grandmother had another stroke. Grandfather had a bad heart, so I took care of her for a few months. While I was there, my mother called her parents. I happened to answer the phone.

My mother told me they, as in her and my real father, had a job babysitting "a cute two year old!" My heart and mind were all of a sudden afraid. That fear I knew as a child was rushing in, but this time, for a helpless little girl I did not know or could not save!

Wrong!

My mother let me know what days they babysat this child and told me, demanded, not call on her off days. Saying they couldn't take personal calls, and they would be in trouble. For two days, all I could think about was that child being afraid in the sense that I remember. Day three had come. I called that number. A woman answered the phone, and I asked for my mother by name. She said that she was not there, and I asked if I could leave a message for my mother. She said, "I'm sorry, she doesn't have any children."

Now I know one reason I was not to call on off days! I continued to describe my mother to her. She was in shock. She wanted to know why on earth she was lied to. So I simply told her, there were five of us. She had lost us because her husband was a child molester. I told her I called to make sure she knew what they were and to protect her child and get her checked by a doctor immediately. She said, "I will protect her, please don't ever call here again." I told her I wouldn't, but if I found out they still watched her child, my next call would be the police. I hung up.

A few days later, my mother called from a different number, collect. They had been fired, and she just could not figure out why. I blasted her, blasted her for allowing him near a child that he could hurt. I yelled at her for the ignorance she showed in this situation. She made me sick, and I told her so. It was okay for her to watch someone else's kid, but she didn't want to take care of her own children? She was again putting another child in harm's way.

We didn't talk again the rest of the summer. That was the first time I really ever showed my real mother disrespect. We would not talk for another year or two. Then one night when they were drunk, she called me. Telling me how horrible life was, and she couldn't take it. She only called when she was drinking. If she found out my father called when she wasn't home, she would get mad at me and ask what we talked about. Even after all of that, I still wanted my parents in my life. It would continue to eat at me, and I would drink again. It was my choice to choose to drink again. I figured if I was going to have them in my life, I needed to stay numb. It was a very sick way of thinking.

It would be another ten years before I saw her. Then she came to visit probably eleven years ago. It was the first time as an adult I had seen her. Her and her third husband would visit for about a week, and it went well. I think we were all in the honeymoon period, so it was considered a success. We decided there could be another visit, and this time, we flew her and her husband to Pennsylvania for Christmas. It was going well until we went to the mall. Her and her husband and our youngest son and my husband were in one store. The girls and I went to another. All of a sudden, I hear my mother yelling, "Chrissy!!! Chrissy!!!"

First of all, my name is *Christy*! Second of all, I am an *adult* with children! I was so embarrassed and mad at her. Unfortunately, for her my emotions are not hidden on my face at all. I can just imagine the look I gave her when I came out of the store. I looked at her and asked what her problem was. I made it very clear I was an adult, and she pronounced my name wrong. I was so unforgiving in that moment. She acted like a child, looked at me, and simply said, "I don't want to lose you again." Lose me again? Seriously? It wasn't like she turned around when I was a child and someone took me, and I wasn't found for years! "She gave me away! She gave me up! She chose a male, an abusive, worthless male over helpless children, her children."

I was so angry.

No, I did not apologize.

I don't think I spoke to her for a few hours, and if I did, she was met with short snappy answers, with the only emotion being anger and distance.

The next day, we made Christmas cookies. And we did the traditions we always do, my family that is. Cookies, music, laughter, it was fun. My mother was actually helping. And then the darn tears started to flow. So with half an attitude, who am I kidding? It was full on attitude. I asked what could possibly be wrong. Again, what could possibly wrong? She was with her daughter and a few of the grandchildren.

She said she was having fun, but she never got to do this with us when we were little kids.

I snapped! I don't think I yelled at her, but I looked at her with hate and disgust in my eyes and heart. My tone was of a parent scolding a child with nothing but hate. My exact words were, "It was your own damn fault you chose not to do things like this. *You* blew it, not me! So stop crying and just try to have fun so you don't ruin it for *my* children!"

As I write this now, wow, what a jerk I was! How hateful and hurtful I was. That woman was feeling a loss and a pain for not being the mother she wished she had been in that moment. And what did I do? I treated her like everyone else in her life did. I wanted her to help, to be a part of the tradition. I wanted to show her I was doing a good job as a parent. That no matter what she did or did not do, I was getting something right.

And it wasn't because of her. My motives became wrong when she started feeling like she was a failure again. I made sure she knew she was a failure. In those few moments, I didn't get it right. I failed big time. I wanted her to know I was in charge, that she could not control anything I did. I hurt her so bad with my words, my facial expressions, my tone, my hateful how dare you be a victim mode in this moment, my moment to shine as a mom. A dull, dark, rusted penny was shining brighter than I was.

For a long time, I was proud of that. I showed her. I showed her that I was unforgiving and could care less how she felt or what she needed. I didn't set a good example for the kids. I taught them that if someone hurts you deep in your heart, don't forgive them and be as malicious as possible. And just because they are ready to show love, it's on your terms only. Yep, I sure showed her. What is also sad is my kids didn't budge when I had my "showed her" moment. They knew I was an angry, hurtful person.

That visit lasted a week, and then she and her husband went to my brother's and sister-in-law's house for the few remaining days of the visit. My mother made it very clear that she no longer drank. Okay, awesome. I wasn't judging her if she wanted to, as that was the talk before they left my house. My brother liked to have New Year's Eve parties. And if she wanted to drink, I honestly didn't care. It wasn't at my house, so whatever. I had been sober for a few years, so it was good.

Well, guess who called on the night of the party? Yep. Can you guess who was trashed and drunk? Yep. Sure enough, my mother was toasted. She had my sister-in-law call me. She tried to warn me before my mother got on the phone. I could have said anything I wanted, and she would not have remembered a single thing. Believe it or not, I didn't say anything mean. I was surprised that she lied. That she was so determined to convince me she didn't drink anymore that I really thought she was telling the truth.

The next afternoon, we had to pick them up to get them on the train back home to Texas. For the thirty-minute ride there, I just kept thinking she lied. Nothing has changed with her. All I could see was how she was always letting me down. As I walked up to the porch,

I could hear every one laughing. I walked in, and they stopped. My brother and his wife just looked at me like they had so much to say but neither spoke. My mother and stepfather said goodbyes; my brother said we would talk later. We left. I must have had the look of choking someone. My husband whispered, "Don't, honey, not now." Let me tell you, I did not listen. Again in the presence of my children, I blew it.

I glanced back and looked at her and asked if she had a headache. She looked mad instantly and asked why I would ask that. "You have a hangover, don't you? That comes from getting drunk the night before!"

She snapped back, "I wasn't drinking! I told you I don't drink anymore!" And of course, stepdad chimes in about not talking to my mother like that and how she was telling the truth, yad-da yad-da yad-da. I tuned him out and literally laughed at her and reminded both of them that I spoke with her on the phone the night before.

There was an awkward and uncomfortable silence the next fifteen minutes to the train station. All I could think was in a few short moments, she would be on the train, and I would be okay. I could be done. I would never have to see or speak to her again. I could kill her in my mind, and that would be it. Never would I have to talk to this lying disappointment of a parent again. There would be no more chances in my lifetime. When we got back to my town and to the train station, I practically jumped out of the van and grabbed their things, telling the kids to say goodbye to the grandparents because they had a long way to go, and we had no idea when we would see them again. Yes, I lied to my kids. We were never going to see them again. I already knew that. I was not going to let my kids get close to this woman just for her to mess it all up again and not be there for them.

Can you guess whose train wasn't coming on time? Yep! Another train derailed, and it was on the tracks, so their train could not get through. Greyhound buses were on the way to get all of the people stranded. It would be *two hours*! *What?!* You have got to be kidding? What are we doing for two hours? I wanted to leave them there and take my family home, far away from her. John said no. I guess I needed to make sure she got on that bus, gone for good I think.

150

We decided to go eat. They wouldn't get out of the van; she was too sick. I didn't care nor did I fight. I asked if she wanted me to get her anything, she ignored me. So I slammed the van door.

Another lesson I taught my children, stoop to their level and be a donkey.

I called my brother. The conversation was very colorful. Full of lies that she told me about my brother and his family. Lies she told my brother about my family and I.

We both agreed that at least we tried, and we didn't need to again. We grew beyond that kind of chaos. We had each other and our families. We didn't need her now after all of these years. I cried. I could hear his voice crack. He said, "It's okay, little sis, I got ya!" We hung up.

My heart hurt so very bad, but I knew I had to say goodbye to her this time for good. And not get sucked back in again. I had to!

Finally, the buses arrived. I said goodbye to her husband with a big whatever attitude as he is going on and on about what a great time he had and he can't wait to do it again. And I must say that I was not kind to him about what I saw with how he treated my mother. I let him know she was not a slave. He was so oblivious with how I felt toward him. I honestly don't know how that is possible.

The time was upon me to say see ya never again. She hugged me, and yes, I hugged her back, hard. I was beginning to mourn her in that very sad moment. She looked at me and said, "I love you, Chrissy."

I almost laughed. I looked at her and said, "You know, it's sad, but I do believe that you do, and I love you, goodbye." I turned and walked away, sobbing. My husband hugged me as we watched the busses go. I was too tired and hurt to be angry. It was so sad as we drove home that the kids were saying how sorry they were for me being hurt and their grandmother not being nice. When we got out of the van, they hugged me as they cried. The only thing I did right was while hugging them, I was saying how much I loved them. And that I would always be there for them.

Weeks later, she called saying she hadn't heard from me, was I okay or was I mad at her? I unleashed on that woman. I screamed at her. I made it very clear I was hurt and angry. Well, she knew I was angry. All she could say was she was an adult, and she didn't have to answer to me. I was just a child and not her keeper. I reminded her adults should know the difference between the truth and a lie. And not only know but admit when they are caught in it. I continued with the day she got on that bus was the day she died. I no longer had a living mother. And I slammed the phone down and sobbed. I got so angry that I wasted tears on her again. She was not worth shedding tears over. My heart was never going to heal from the scars, and now it was broken again and again.

What I taught my oldest daughter who happened to be home that morning was that if I made her angry, she could scream at me and tell me how much she hated me. How worthless I was and how I never listened to her and that she could pronounce me dead from her life with just a few words spoken. Trust me when I say I taught her well because she has done just that a time or two.

I used to joke around about how dumb I thought my mother was. How childlike she was. I would compare her to a happy meal. The drink was spilled, the nuggets half-cooked and some missing, the fries cold and soggy, and the toy broken. Basically, she was a broken mess I wanted nothing to do with. Oh, the laughs that would come from me when I spoke this analogy.

It wasn't until God changed my heart that I realized I was angry at her because I was hurting. I was hurting because she was not a mother to me. She was not a mother to me because she didn't know how to be. Not that it makes it all okay, it does not. She abandoned me. She didn't stand up for me. I was hurt. I didn't care that she was wounded. Making her feel my wrath was more important than caring for her pain. Not caring for her pain kept me safe and unbreakable. Little did I know just how broken I had already been.

God has shown me how my wrath doesn't help either of us. I can be angry with her or feel hurt without striking out like a badger.

> For all have sinned and fall short of the glory of
> God. (Romans 3:23, NIV)

Therefore, since we have been justified through faith, we have peace with God through our Lord Jesus Christ, through whom we have gained access by faith into this grace in which we now stand. And we boast in the hope of the glory of God. Not only so, but we also glory in our sufferings, because we know suffering produces perseverance; perseverance, character; and character, hope. And hope does not put us to shame, because God's love has been poured out into our hearts through the Holy Spirit, who has been given to us. You see, at just the right time, when we were still powerless, Christ died for the ungodly. Very rarely will anyone die for a righteous person, though for a good person someone might possibly dare to die. But God demonstrates his own love for us in this: while we were still sinners, Christ died for us. (Romans 5:1–8, NIV)

"The time has come," he said. "The kingdom of God has come near. Repent and believe the good news!" (Mark 1:15, NIV)

Lord, I am sorry for the hurt I added to her life. May she, one day, forgive me as you have.

Responses

1. No. (11)
2. Yes. (18)
3. Oh my, yeah, I guess I could be a smart-mouthed creature on an occasion or two.
4. When she was sick and asked me to do something I didn't want to do.
5. Not sure I ever did.
6. Yes, when my marriage fell apart.
7. Not that I can remember.
8. Only once. (2)
9. Yes, in my teen years. (5)
10. Yes, but we were taught to respect our parents and elders at all times. If I was mad, it had to come out later.
11. Yes, when she placed herself in a situation between my sister and I.
12. When she was overbearing when I was a teenager. She just wanted me to be safe.
13. Far too many times. (4)
14. I'm sure there was! (2)
15. Yes, and she forgave me.
16. Yep! If she complains, I get tired of it quickly.
17. Many times but it never lasted long.
18. I would have gotten smacked!
19. Yes, during our discussion about Catholics versus Protestants.
20. More times than I want to admit. But she always forgave me.
21. When she was sick and didn't want to fight anymore.
22. Way too many to count.
23. When my father passed away.
24. Yes, when I had wanted my freedom and independence after graduating college.
25. Really?
26. When she wants forgiveness and I'm not ready for that yet.

27. One thing I hate about myself when my mom was alive was, I was always angry with her. There are too many times when I should have shown her mercy instead of wrath that I can't even just name one time.
28. She was always angry.
29. When she locks her keys in her car.
30. When she tried to have my oldest son call her Mom because she was embarrassed to have a fifteen-year-old with a baby.
31. When she left.
32. As an adult, yes, sometimes but not like I really wanted to. I owed her my opinion! But I did not do as she did! I did *not* want to be that kind of person! I vowed to myself I would *never be like my mother!* I am not either!
33. I am ashamed to say yes, and I'll never forget. I called her a B in a physical fight. She hits like a man she does.
34. More than I should have.
35. She slapped my face after I had done wrong.
36. In her recent divorce. She's 75.
37. No, but I should have.
38. Too many times. I can be a bit of a hothead, and I try not to take it out on others, but sometimes, she happens to be on the receiving end because I spend so much time with her. But she also helps me to work through my anger and figure out why because nine out of ten times, it is misdirected.
39. LOL.
40. After my parents divorced, I was rebellious and wild.
41. Yes, I often took my anger out on her.
42. Whenever I didn't talk to her for years after she had an affair that split our family.
43. Teen angst (fifteen to seventeen) where I didn't want her help or to hear her reasoning to anything.
44. I've lost my patience a couple of times when I should not have. Depression can be frustrating.
45. During all of my pregnancies when I would flip out before thinking. Or when it came to a family member I cared about, and we would disagree what was best for them.

46. Sadly, yes.

47. Yes, more than I care to remember. We forget that mothers are only human too.

48. Planning my wedding—I was so selfish.

49. I'm sure, when she wanted me to do something and I was an angry teen wanting to do something else. I don't remember ever physically acting out in anger though. Maybe yelling, but my mother would have stopped that real quick. Ha-ha-ha.

50. Right before she died, I wasn't nice to her and told her that her surgery was not a big deal, but she died from it.

51. One time at dinner, I was talking to my mom about a career. I had to be about sixteen or seventeen. My mom said she was a stay-home mom, that's a career. I said in the snottiest tone I could muster, "Oh, Mother, you're so archaic (earlier times)." Ironically, after I had children, I was a stay-at-home mom. That was as close to wrath as I've given. I was afraid of my parents.

52. Her migraines.

53. Honestly, probably more than I should have!

54. Teen years, when I thought I knew it all, just leave me alone and don't bring my friends into this as I came to realize what a jerk I was.

55. Too many! When I was drinking and drugging.

56. Once but I almost immediately apologized.

57. Yes, when she abused me mentally and verbally in front of my kids and said it was my fault.

58. Lots of times! I should have been hog tied and beat. I was impatient with her and didn't always speak kindly.

59. When she would call me and all she would do is complain about everything and make herself sound really bad and there's nothing that can be done or just real bad in general. I would get mad and just hang up on her and say the call dropped or lost service.

60. Probably not. Sometimes, I needed to support my wife when she had a different idea from my mom.

61. I don't know if I would use the word *wrath*, there are plenty of times that I have snapped at her or just been short with her when I should have been patient or understanding of her perspective. Maybe there are moments I showed wrath, but I can't really think of any in particular.

Now it's your turn to answer.

Is there a time when you showed your mother wrath instead of mercy?

_____
_____
_____
_____
_____
_____
_____
_____
_____
_____
_____
_____
_____
_____
_____
_____
_____
_____
_____
_____
_____
_____
_____
_____

Chapter 16

A Moment She Showed Mercy When You Should Have Seen Wrath

I have struggled with this section with deep pain and fear of the truth. I understand a portion of this pain, but some I do not. This is about my mother showing mercy toward me instead of anger, wrath, and action. It is truly nothing I did. But I was the result of her pain. I have had a song playing continuously to get the courage of this chapter. I still don't have it, but God is with me as He always has been. Part of the song says I just let go and I feel so exposed.

I haven't even gotten to the toughest part, and I am crushed already. Please be patient with me as I walk this road. I want many rabbit trails to nowhere. But that will get me nowhere near where I need to be. I want to skip this. Please know I am not trying to hurt you, Mom. I need to do this.

I feel sick, afraid of upsetting others, of not walking completely through this to heal.

Lord, I'm ready now . . .

I have been through many things my mother had gone through. I'm not bragging or trying to outdo her. Her life is not one I ever wanted to practice, repeat, or perfect.

I have to give a little history of a choice of mine that created pain that no one needs to deal with before I get to my mother's mercy toward me.

I was out at a friend's apartment drinking and smoking pot. Things were going what I thought was good. Yes, I know how that

159

sounds. There were four of us there that night, my friend, her boy-friend, and a friend of theirs. We all hung out in the living room for about an hour I think. The other couple went to their bedroom and things started to get serious with who I was with. I had never met him until that night. When I drank or got high, nothing mattered. I was reckless and careless with my time and life. We had been kissing, and it went too fast, and we were no longer on the couch. We were on the living room floor, and he was on top of me. I can recall the weight of his body. I can hear his voice and feel his breath in my ear. I remember saying stop. I said no so many times. I was high; I couldn't make him stop. He was raping me, and I couldn't make him stop. I was hurting and in pain; there was nothing to grab ahold of. I couldn't get away. No matter how many times I said no or cried out, hoping my friend would hear, he just continued raping me. All I could do was cry and look to the front door. I could see the light of the hallway to the outside door and other apartments. I cried as he continued. When he was done, he got up, kissed me, and said thanks. I got up and pulled my clothing on and walked out the door to my apartment in the next building over and got in the shower. All I could do was blame myself for what just happened.

I was high. I didn't make him stop. I didn't beat the crap out of him. I didn't defend myself. I let him do this to me! Those thoughts just kept playing in my head for so many hours (actually years). I don't know how long I was in the shower. I didn't sleep at all.

When I finally realized the sun was up, I started cleaning my apartment. It wasn't even dirty, but I remember thinking what else do I do? I can't get clean, maybe I can clean where I live then I won't feel so dirty.

It must have been around noon when someone knocked on my door. I opened it. It was him, the one who wouldn't listen to me, the one who didn't stop. I blamed myself anyways, and I thought that I had nothing else to lose. He just walked past me like nothing happened, and I let him. Again, I did not stop him, but I was sober and still afraid. He had a container in his hand that was full of fruit punch and 100-proof whiskey. I remember the color because of the stain it made on his white jeans. I was not turning my back on him, but I was trying to figure out how to get him out without getting hurt. If you saw his eyes, you would know that no one was home. On top of that, he was drinking.

God, I feel so dirty again. Give me strength, I don't care how much I cry or how hard the tears fall. Give me enough courage to continue, to finish this.

He started talking again like nothing was wrong. I don't even know what he said to me; I just know that at the sound of his voice, I cringed. He was so arrogant and comfortable with his actions. He knew I wouldn't report him.

He wanted a glass for his drink. I got it for him, and he poured the mix into the glass. I watched it, and I figured it out. A few drops fell, so I started cleaning it up and knocked the glass over. It went everywhere all over him and his white jeans. He grabbed my wrist so hard that it took all I had not to scream. All of a sudden, I had strength or enough unfogged fear that I allowed him to pull me close as he was sitting. I was in his face, threatening to take every part of what made him a man apart if he didn't leave. I let him know he would never touch me again, and he would never rape me again. I shoved him out of my apartment with such force and slammed and locked the door. I sat on the floor crying for I don't know how long, but he was gone. He was right about me not reporting him.

I was twenty when that happened, and I am almost forty-six. It has taken me years to finally realize it was not my fault. Could I have made better choices and not been drinking or smoking weed? Yes, I could have. But no is no, and my actions do not make it okay!

I still cringe and feel very dirty when I think about it or talk about it. His name makes me sick, and when I would see him or even his twin brother, I was on edge and panicked. I won't ever have to worry about seeing him again; he is dead. I'm not sure how and I don't care. Thank God, he will not hurt another woman. I found out I was not the first. And if there were others after me, I am so sorry that I did not report it. I'm sorry.

National Sexual Abuse Hotline Number 1-800-656-4673

A little over forty-six years ago, my mother was raped. She was violated by a man that she trusted, and I believe in her eyes, loved.

He took from her something she can never get back. Like I said in a previous chapter, that is when she got pregnant with me. So are you wondering what this has to do with her showing me mercy and not wrath?

She did not abort me when she found out she was pregnant. I don't know if that has to do with the laws in the 70's or her feelings on abortion, considering I would be the fourth child.

I know that life has been tough in so many ways, but had she shown wrath for the pain she suffered through, I would not be here. She gave me the chance to take a breath and live. She gave me the chance to grow and struggle, the chance to mess up and learn. She gave me a life that would be difficult, but it was life. It's not her fault for every little or big thing I went through.

By letting me live, I have children, sons-in-law, and grandchildren. I am an aunt, a friend, a sister. I have a wonderful husband who loves me, no matter what baggage I have or the damage and self-sabotaging things I have done. I know the voice of God because I have a personal relationship with Jesus! No matter what the reason for continuing the pregnancy, she did it. I can understand to a little degree why she did drugs and drank while pregnant with me. I used to be so angry for her doing that. Now that I know the truth and know she did not have any support, I kind of understand. I'm not angry at her for it anymore. I don't condone it and wouldn't want others to do drugs or drink while pregnant. I am just thankful she didn't end the pregnancy.

I get to live and share the good news of what God has to say to all of you! I get the chance to speak of His love for you and let you know you are not alone in the pains and the hurts of this world. I get to tell you that there is hope and salvation, and I get to tell you why I know this to be true.

"'Go, stand in the temple courts,' he said, 'and tell the people all about this new life'" (Acts 5:20, NIV).

I get to do that because of my mother because she made a choice not to take her wrath out on me. I don't know if she ever loved me, but she sure gave me nine months of mercy!

At daybreak they entered the temple courts, as they had been told, and began to teach the people. (Acts 5:21, NIV)

Consider it pure joy, my brothers and sisters, whenever you face trials of many kinds, because you know that the testing of your faith produces perseverance. Let perseverance finish its work so that you may be mature and complete, not lacking anything. (James 1:2–4, NIV)

Blessed is the one who perseveres under trial because, having stood the test, that person will receive the crown of life that the Lord has promised to those who love him. (James 1:12, NIV).

But in your hearts revere Christ as Lord. Always be prepared to give an answer to everyone who asks you to give the reason for the hope that you have. But do this with gentleness and respect. (1 Peter 3:15, NIV)

Responses

1. She found out I was pregnant at eighteen.
2. When she didn't swing the cast iron skillet at my head a second time after I ducked the first time.
3. Oh my, probably more times than I have any idea. She was a good disciplinarian; there was order in our home. But once when I was a teenager, I had done something thoughtless and forgot a special day. It hurt her very much, but she didn't tell me till later.
4. One time I took the Buick without permission.
5. She found out I spent the night at a friend's house, and we were out all night.
6. Multiple times when I disobeyed her or my father's wishes.
7. She'd show mercy first, but eventually her wrath would come out.
8. She wasn't much for mercy.
9. Losing and breaking glasses growing up.
10. The night I left home and moved in with my now husband, she begged me to stay.
11. It always upset me much more when she would just look at me sadly and quietly rather than get angry.
12. When she caught me smoking.
13. There were many. I thought she would be very upset when I said I was pregnant and unmarried. She was kind, loving, and took care of me.
14. Never, it was wrath.
15. Never. (3)
16. When we deserved mercy, we go mercy.
17. When I let the entire milk tank run down the drain of the milk house.
18. When I was sixteen, seeing an older man.
19. When dating the wrong man.
20. When I don't hold my tongue all of the time.
21. When I partied too hard in high school.
22. When I told her about having sex.

23. Anytime I broke one of her collectibles. She would be upset, but she didn't put their importance above mine.
24. When I ran away at five.
25. When I got married.
26. Not often enough.
27. Too many to mention.
28. I used to get in trouble for disobeying, but she was never mean to me for it.
29. When I was going through grief at the loss of my husband.
30. When she found out how sick she was and said this is the path God chose for her.
31. Stupid things I did as a teen.
32. During my divorce.
33. When I was a horribly mouthy teenager.
34. When she cleaned my knee after I fell where she told me not to go.
35. When I lied to her and she knew I was lying but couldn't prove it.
36. When I got pregnant. (2)
37. When I got caught shoplifting when I was ten.
38. When I left home.
39. When she caught me drinking the first time.
40. My husband went through depression many years ago and acted out in anger once. My mom showed more concern than anger.
41. Bad mother.
42. My mom didn't speak much English, and her employer used to cheat them from overtime money. Our family didn't have much money and she needed a job, so she allowed them to get away with it.
43. When I got caught skipping class.
44. She hasn't.
45. When I glued the wall.
46. When I was fifteen and pregnant.
47. When I would get smart.
48. When I was a teenage and got drunk.

49. When she found out I miscarried in school. It's still a secret few know. I wasn't always a great kid, and I held a lot of anger and resentment. Now I know as a mother, it wasn't her fault. She showed kindness and love and compassion. Lord, I was so sad and scared. She never once screamed at me. But said God has a plan for everyone, and things happen for a reason.

50. At sixteen when I told her I was pregnant. (2)

51. I ran away from home.

52. When I came home drunk one night when I was eighteen.

53. When I got pregnant out of wedlock. (2)

54. She never showed mercy on me.

55. When my dad was drunk.

56. When I punched my stepmom's niece and called her a —— after she pushed me off the monkey bars. She told me I was being harder on myself than she could be on me because I told on myself and gave myself an anxiety attack.

57. Daily.

58. When she didn't tell my dad on me for something I did.

59. My mother is and was not very merciful.

60. I never saw my mother show wrath.

61. She is full of grace.

62. When I broke her fine china.

63. When I tried to skip school in high school.

64. Sorry, it was always wrath.

65. Failing my first college class.

66. Every day of my life. Ha-ha.

67. Always. I know when I disappointed her, but she never so much as raised her voice. She did not have to.

68. The time I backed into a car.

69. More times than I deserved as a teenager.

70. When I took off and nobody knew where I went.

71. When I acted like I deserved better than I truly did.

72. Never lost her cool with me.

73. When I ran away numerous times.

74. Probably holding back info from my dad to keep me from getting into more trouble.
75. When I told a secret.
76. When I threw a massive drinking party while she was out of town. I didn't even get grounded, let alone yelled at, so calm it was scary.
77. All through my drinking and drugging years, sixteen to thirty-four, always by my side.
78. When I got caught shoplifting and she had to take me to Logan Township Police for fingerprinting.
79. When I was a teenager and was grounded for smoking cigarettes, she would lie to my stepdad to keep me from getting in more trouble.
80. Yes, Mom gave her ornery son many grace times. Dad was a no nonsense, discipline, hard work, and in church every time the doors were open, man.
81. When I was abused.
82. She has softened and grown over the years. Certain things she would have freaked out over before are now handled with more grace.

Now it's your turn to answer.

When was a moment she showed mercy when you should have seen wrath?

_____

_____

_____

_____

_____

_____

_____

_____

_____

_____

_____

_____

_____

_____

_____

_____

_____

_____

_____

_____

_____

_____

_____

_____

_____

_____

_____

_____

Chapter 17

Was There a Time When You Showed Mercy When You Wanted to Show Wrath?

I am not sure how to answer this question.

Mercy: (1) kind and gentle treatment of a wrongdoer; (2) a kind sympathetic disposition; willingness to forgive, spare, or help; (3) a blessing as an act of divine love.

Wrath: violent anger; rage.

Wrathful: (1) full of wrath, (2) showing wrath

There were times I wanted to be kind and gentle, to be sympathetic and forgive, and a few times, I wanted to help her. And we know from a few chapters back that I had plenty of anger and rage toward her.

When she had the stroke that took my sister and I down south for a few days, I was not thrilled about going. I didn't want to go, but I wasn't going to let my sister who hadn't talked to or seen her in thirty plus years go alone. I couldn't do that to my sister. We flew into two separate airports, and my sister could not get a rental car. It wasn't her fault; I really believe that God had things He wanted to show her. But it wasn't going to happen if she had to lead. She needed to be the passenger to see what was happening. So I land in Louisiana and her in Texas, about forty minutes away from each other. She also landed an hour before me, so she can't get a rental in this dinky airport, and they lose her luggage. So far, the trip is going horribly wrong for her. I land, make a few phone calls as she did, and I get the rental. Praising God, calling my sis, and telling her I am on

169

my way. I get into the car and adjusting everything to fit my short legs and I find K-LOVE radio station in Louisiana! Again, praising God for that gift in my travels! I get to my sister and so very glad to see her and hug her. We or I decided to just get this started and go straight to the nursing home where our mother was. We got lost or at least stuck in the "loop." My GPS wanted to go another way than hers, and since I was driving, I told her to just hold on and see where it took us. So here we are at a stop sign in a nice quiet place, and she says, "Look, it's a police officer! Let's see if he knows where this place is." We wait for him and tell him we are from out of town, can't find the nursing home, and does he know where this place is.

I kid you not, his response was a pure God moment. He looks at us and says, "Let me lead you!" Who says that? What police officer says, "Let me lead you?" An angel from God so my sister can see Him in the whole situation! As the officer turned around, my sister and I just look at each other and say "let me lead you" at the same time! I told her that was a God moment. She said, "No, that was baby Jesus!" LOL.

We made a few turns, and we were right where we passed ten plus times! We drove right past this place so many times and the sign was not seen by either of us. At this point, I think we are still talking about how the officer led us.

If she had gotten the rental, not known about K-LOVE, been driving, would we have been led by God on that trip? Would she have seen God at work? Would we have been as calm as we were when we got to our mother? Would either one of us had compassion for her? I don't think I would have because my goal was to protect my sister at whatever cost from any pain that may come her way. Those two had not spoken for thirty plus years; we also had no idea what her health was really like.

I believe with all my heart that God was in everything with that trip. Without him, my heart would have been so cold toward her. As we learned the things like I said before about her pregnancy, pictures, my sister's wrist, of course, I was hurt and angry and totally confused with all of my emotions. I didn't let it show toward her at all. We laughed and cried a little bit; my sister forgave our mother.

Our mother said she was sorry to her, not for specifics, but that she was sorry mainly for not being there. That was huge, so I had to put my frustration and anger and hurt and moments I thought I might "lose it" aside.

She needed compassion, not just because she had a stroke with minimal affects or damage, but because she also had hurts like us. She suffered at the hands of many, and those many hands that hurt her did not need to include mine again. Not even words spoken were cruel or unkind, and I had moments to speak them. I praise God for keeping my mouth shut.

> My dear brothers and sisters, take note of this: Everyone should be quick to listen, slow to speak and slow to become angry, because human anger does not produce the righteousness that God desires. Therefore, get rid of all moral filth and the evil that is so prevalent and humbly accept the word planted in you, which can save you. (James 1:19–21, NIV)

> Fools give full vent to their rage, but the wise bring calm in the end. (Proverbs 29:11, NIV)

> Do you see someone who speaks in haste? There is more hope for a fool than for them. (Proverbs 29:20, NIV)

> An angry person stirs up conflict, and a hot-tempered person commits many sins. (Proverbs 29:22, NIV)

Did I have some time later, out of our mother's presence, that I dealt with the emotions and information I heard? Yes, I did, and a few people heard from me after we were done visiting, after my sister and I had the chance to talk about some of it. I was so thankful and praising God for the ability to talk to those I needed to in the moments following. The phone closed the distance that the miles created.

Even after going back the next day to see her, we didn't show the emotions we shared with each other. I believe God did that in us. He kept us from spewing any hurt toward her. I was ready to run as maybe my sister was. But I know we did not show that to our mother. We saw a woman wounded and hurting from scars that lived within her heart and mind. We saw her weakened physically by a stroke. In some ways, like I said before, her mind of a child's wanting to tell the secrets that she probably swore to take to the grave. She would never tell us the things she did with a clear mind. Even when I have begged her to tell me things or talk about our childhood, she wouldn't. I know that God got us through it and her as well.

Responses

1. No. (14)
2. Yes. (17)
3. Always. (2)
4. Never.
5. Yes, but I was scared if I stuck around, I would get the skillet swung at me again, so I showed mercy out of self-preservation.
6. Probably different times.
7. Showed her mercy, all the time, when I should have been outraged by her behavior.
8. Yes, many times. (4)
9. Yes, I have turned the other cheek but not as much as I should.
10. Yes, I feared my mom.
11. When she had problems with alcohol and I would take care of her.
12. When she found out a family secret was really true, and I had not lied years beforehand. She said I was an adult now and that I needed to get over it.
13. I respected her.
14. Yes, there was once when I found her with someone other than my daddy.
15. By forgiving her for staying married for seven years to her abusive husband.
16. Yep, held my tongue and consoled.
17. There was one time that she got to do something that meant a lot to me and she didn't let me do it, she did it.
18. Too often during my teenage years.
19. Not really.
20. No, I show respect.
21. When she was going through her grief.
22. Four days before she died, I realized I was being selfish, and when she said I'm tired, I don't want to do this anymore and I hugged and kissed her and said you don't have to.

23. Yes, once.
24. When my mom took my dad's side about an issue that we had, although neither my dad nor I were right.
25. When she left my father.
26. Yes, when she abandoned me and chose to stay with her sex-offender husband.
27. Really?
28. When she told my son that I'm not a good mom because I don't let her see him anytime she wants. I just let it slide and explained to him later that is just her opinion.
29. My parents were going to move in with my sister, but the plan didn't work out, so I allowed them to stay with me. It was supposed to be short term, but it became permanent which I think damaged our relationship. I wished I had put my foot down and not let them stay with me.
30. Often, counseled for anger management.
31. When she dropped my son off at a friend's house, not knowing that he was getting his drugs there.
32. Most every day. Yet trying to explain gently why things were as they were.
33. No, not really. She suffers from mental illness, now mainly PTSD. So a lot of conversations I was getting spoken to like a child and yelled at for my past, or my past drinking issues, and it stung like a knife because for years I've been good, got the help I needed so I could be a better mother and person in general. Just had to let her say her piece and know she needed to clear her mind in order to heal in some ways.
34. Probably so.
35. When my mother couldn't take it that her child was suicidal.
36. Never wanted to show wrath, only once and immediately regretted it.
37. Keeping her a part of my life even though she's hurt me deeply.
38. Summers home from college.

39. Whenever she took over my wedding.

40. Twenties, where I see her struggling with me becoming an adult, so I try to ease it anyway I can.

41. Yes, when I was twelve and she told me that she had an affair. I never got mad or acted out. I said that I forgave her, even if I was not sure what exactly that would entail at that age.

42. Yes, we had a horrible incident happen that pushed me away from her. I was in the right (for once), and I was so very angry and hurt with her for how she handled the situation. But when she finally saw that truth of the situation, she apologized and I forgave her, even though I never intended to when I envisioned her apology.

43. The night before she passed away, when I wanted to scream at her for not calling the doctor when she was having a bad reaction to the medicine change.

44. A lot of times I *should have*, instead, I said nothing.

45. Now, sometimes when she won't listen and reach out to us for help, not really wrath but frustration.

46. When she was crying because of something I did.

47. Yes, many times. Sometimes, my mom makes me very angry. I always bite my tongue because I know she means well, but her depression gets the better of her.

48. When she talked down about my dad cause we weren't allowed to go against her.

49. Never wanted to show Mom wrath. She was a precious gift from God!

50. When she put me down in front of people.

51. There have been times when I felt highly misunderstood. When I was younger, there were moments where I wanted to scream about it to make her realize I didn't think she was really listening. I wouldn't say I showed mercy in those moments—I probably saved myself a few groundings by keeping my mouth shut. After those angry moments, I would think about if I had yelled and how that would have made her feel. I think I've always known that she was inse-

cure about her parenting abilities and wanting to be better than her own mom. I never wanted to make her feel like she was a bad mom.

Now it's your turn to answer.

Was there a time when you showed mercy when you wanted to show wrath?

_____
_____
_____
_____
_____
_____
_____
_____
_____
_____
_____
_____
_____
_____
_____
_____
_____
_____
_____
_____
_____
_____
_____
_____
_____
_____

Chapter 18

What Makes a Good Mom?

Here are a few things I found under the word *good*: satisfactory, helpful, kind, behaving well, being honest and upright, showing good sense or good judgment, better than average and something good.

Yes, I believe that is a decent start to what qualities a good mom should have in her tool box of parenting.

Let's see what is under mom or mother: mother, a female parent, being in the relationship of a mother to others, and to be or act as a mother.

So I would think we could agree that a mother is a person who has a special relationship with whom she mothers. I found it kind of funny that it says to act as a mother. There is no further definition to mother, so how does one act like a mother? Must we put another word in front of it like the question of what makes a good mom? We then look up good as we did and assume every woman who becomes a mom acts this way.

Of course, that is what I want to assume. Though I know that to be false because not every mom is like this. Wouldn't it be wonderful if it were true? Of course, it would. But this world is full of pain and uncaring mothers, with children, small or grown, hurting or angry because those actions of being good were not followed enough.

I am guilty as well of this happening in my own family. I think that our life's experiences also determine what we believe makes a good mom.

In just one example to see what a good mom is we will go to Scripture.

Two prostitutes who lived in the same home both had children. One woman lay on her son and he died. In the middle of the night, she switched babies with the other woman. So they take their problem to King Solomon, and with no other witnesses to what had happened, this is what the king said.

> The King said, "This one says, 'My son is alive and your son is dead,' while that one says, 'No! Your son is dead and mine is alive.'" Then the king said, "Bring me a sword." So they brought a sword for the king, He then gave an order: "Cut the living child in two and give half to one and half to the other." The woman whose son was alive was deeply moved out of love for her son and said to the king, "Please, my lord, give her the living baby! Don't kill him!" But the other said, "Neither I nor you shall have him. Cut him in two!" Then the king gave his ruling: "Give the living baby to the first woman. Do not kill him; she is his mother." (1 Kings 3:23–27, NIV)

This mother was willing to sacrifice raising her son for him to stay alive. She would allow another woman to hold and care for him to save him.

Can we agree that goes in the good mom category?

So we still have the question of what makes a good mom. What makes a mom good? I believe it is taking care of herself from day one when she finds out she is pregnant. I know that is an obvious statement. I'm sure we all know at least one pregnant gal that made not so great choices. If not, you do now. I was not the best at making good decisions when I was pregnant with my first two babies. I drank some with the first, didn't eat totally healthy, and the stress was ridiculous. Emotionally, my first pregnancy was torture with the way my first husband acted. There was a lot of emotional and verbal abuse for most of the nine months. I was really blessed that my daughter was healthy with knowing today how bad stress and the things I did can affect an unborn baby.

I loved her so much, and I thought she would keep me sane. A baby can't do that. One thing that would have made a difference is a support system as a sixteen-year-old getting pregnant and seventeen being a new mom. I know I did not have that.

My second pregnancy was worse with horrible choices. I didn't eat right, and I was often bouncing from one place to another. My first child was with her father, and this baby was not his. I had left him a few times already before I got pregnant. After I left him, I was doing drugs, drinking all the time, and sleeping around to get what I needed. Yes, what I am saying is I was selling my body for these things, food, money, car rides, or a place to just sleep for a while. I went to Florida with a trucker I met right after hanging up the public phone I was on. After not get the response I wanted from the other end of the phone, it didn't really matter because I had nowhere to go. I was homeless. That was one of the many genius things I did during this time. This was going on for the first three months of the pregnancy. I ended up going back to the first child's father. Being pregnant and homeless was getting tiring. I wanted to keep this baby, and he said he would help. His mother was another story because we lived with her. But I wanted to be with my little girl and try and take care of the one I was carrying. So I caved in and did whatever my future ex-husband wanted. I figured it was okay because I was using him so I could be with my little girl.

When my second little girl was born, it was an extremely rough delivery for both of us. The cord was wrapped around her throat, and I almost bleed out. I held her. I loved her but she would not be going back into the hell I feel like I created.

A little less than twenty-four hours after giving birth to my sweet baby, I signed adoption papers. That little girl would go home with another mommy and daddy. She would be loved and held by someone else. She wouldn't have to worry about getting fed or clean diapers. She would be safe from all of my chaos.

Her new mommy wanted it to be an open adoption, and I agreed. It was so much harder than I ever thought. I thought I could turn my emotions on and off like any other day. I was so very wrong. How would I explain to my little girl at home that her sister would not live with us? No one cared when I got home that my heart was broken and a part of me died. They all expected me to get over it because she was not my future ex-husband's, and I didn't have to worry about her since someone else was doing what I couldn't. Yes, those are things I heard after I signed the adopting papers.

I made it clear I didn't want to hear from her new parents or I would change my mind. All they had to do was ignore me or forget me for the next six months. And then the adoption would be final, and they could stop worrying if I would show up one day to take her from them.

There were questions the judge had, so the new mommy had to call me. I asked her how the baby was and what was wrong with her the night before. She asked why, and I told her I heard her crying. Silence.

Then she said that she was up sick and crying; they thought it was an ear infection I believe. That was the only time I heard from her until the day after the adoption was final. After the six months was up and the adoption was final is when we began communicating.

It wasn't long before I left my ex-husband for the last time, taking our child with me. I couldn't deal with his hateful words or demands. I couldn't take that I had given my second baby girl up. The only time I smiled was when I was with my little girl, so we just left.

So out of those times, was I a good mom all the time? Absolutely, not all the time! I didn't handle stress well when my first had colic from 10:00 p.m. to 8:00 a.m. And it was only few weeks, but it felt like a lifetime. Okay, so I got through that but had another child that was not my first husband's. That's not making the right choice for my children. I love both of them, and I would not trade them for anything!

But drinking and all of the things I did with the second pregnancy? How is that a mom of the year award recipient?

Was I always a horrible mom? I think I was, most of the time. I was nowhere near a good mom on a daily basis. All the times, I was out partying and forgot where my daughter was. She doesn't remember the things she saw or heard, or how she would throw temper tantrums because she couldn't handle the life I was raising her in. She doesn't remember seeing me drag down the stairs of our house by her father because I was sick from drinking. How he pulled me down fifteen steps, and I got sick at the bottom, and he put my face in it as I passed out and left me there. She doesn't remember hearing me scream because he was breaking a five-foot mirror by our bed, where her and I sat, all because I didn't want sex.

Or the time I was trying to get away from an ex-boyfriend, and he pulled me up the stairs by my long hair as she stood at the top crying because he was hurting me. I remember the look in her eyes, the fear that I want to forget. That's not the actions of a good mom. Or the time when she had a tantrum and the live-in guy couldn't handle it and beat her butt. I could hear him hit her, and by the time I got through her bedroom door, she was bruising. She doesn't know I went after him and damaged my hand, missing his face, on a brick wall. She doesn't remember me taking her to the hospital and the state police to press charges against him for child abuse. I'm so glad she doesn't.

I praise God that I'm not like that anymore. She doesn't remember me being away for a month because I was in my second drug rehab. What she does know is I am not like that now.

I had plenty of opportunity to attend all of the parties and big days the second child had that I missed. Some I didn't go to because my heart was broken, and I didn't know how to talk about it. Sometimes, I didn't want to be around her parents because I felt unworthy of the time they tried to give me. I always feared they looked at me with disgust in their hearts or like they made a mistake keeping it an open adoption. I felt like this uneducated crack whore had no business being in their nice house or involved in their daughter's life. My insecurities were always making the decisions in my life with her. Not being able to hold her or raise her was just another reason I stayed high or drunk. I used my choice to keep her out of my hell as punishment. People told me I did a great thing by giving her up; I didn't believe it. I just wanted to hold her and watch the girls grow up together. I couldn't handle it, so I stayed numb causing more damage. I'm not saying the only reason I drank or stayed high was because of giving my baby up. There were plenty of reasons before that point in my life; I used to stay cold and numb.

So what situation makes me a worse mother? Both of them do; it doesn't matter the reason or the why. The fact is simple. I messed up in a huge way with both of them. That's what my heart and my mind tell me.

Those were moments I totally blew it out of the water for bad parent of the day, week, month, and year award. Did I really mess up that bad? Yes, I did. Where there times I got it right? Yes, I believe there are a few.

Times when I would hold my little girl when she had a bad dream, kiss her boo-boos, hold her hand when walking down the sidewalk, give her healthy food, play with her or snuggle while watching cartoons. Yes, I got those moments right. I was a good mom then. She had my full attention and was safe.

What about when I took my little girl to see her sister and watch them grow and form a bond? How about going to gymnastics because my daughter wanted her friends to meet her birth mom and her big sister? And when we got there, she tripped and hurt her knee, and I picked her up. She was crying, and she says, "I want my mommy." And I hand her over to her "mommy"! Did I get it right? Yes, I did. Was I a good mom then? I want to say yes, I was, and it hurt so very bad. My heart was in so much pain I thought it would crack in half right there. I held in the tears and the pain to protect myself from being seen as weak and failing.

Fortunately for them, I continued to get it right. There were still sticks along the way to trip over. Even though there are sticks to trip over, both of those girls are great mommies! I am so proud of who they are and how far they have come!

I sit here after writing this, and I have to say I don't think my mom was a good parent either. I think the fact that as we were older and she could have that contact, she didn't want it or seek after us.

That's probably why I don't think she was ever a good mother. You can't be called a good mom when you don't want your kids.

I know that sounds horrible and judgmental after everything I just told you. I am probably comparing her bad to mine and thinking that at least I protected my kids. Who am I trying to kid? Yes, I know what I told you and not a whole lot of that says protection, does it? Can I tell you I am really struggling with this right now? I wish I could paint a beautiful picture of me being the most caring mom and making all the right choices and always having my feet planted firm on a solid foundation. But I cannot do that.

I was behaving like my own mother. She didn't take care of herself being pregnant with me, high and drinking as well. Being with my father was not healthy either. I think there were some times she got it right but not many that I know of. She has met a few of the grandchildren, but none of us sent our children to Grandmas for a weekend. None of us would ever do that. I'm lucky my grandchildren come to my house.

If you have struggled like me or others, please don't hang your head. You can try to get it right. Yes, it is going to take time, but it starts with the desire to want it.

So let's forget about the definition of good according to the dictionary for a few moments. There are so many times we are out and about in our communities where we see examples of what we believe to be good or bad. What I see may not be bad to me, but to you, it could be the worst thing ever. I believe discipline is extremely important, discipline, not abuse. If not, we have these unruly, disrespecting kids running around, causing all kinds of trouble and pain. Then they grow up to be horrible people, trying to act like adults. Children need to be disciplined. They need and want to be taught right from wrong.

> Whoever spares the rod hates their children, but the one who loves their children is careful to discipline them. (Proverbs 13:24, NIV)

Those who spare the rod of discipline hate their children. Those who love their children care enough to discipline them. (Proverbs 13:24, NLT)

The one who spares his rod hates his child, but the one who loves his child is diligent in disciplining him. (Proverbs 13:24, NET)

He who spares his rod hates his son, but he who loves him disciplines him promptly. (Proverbs 13:24, NKJV)

I don't think these verses are just about spanking but disciplining our children so they learn and grow. I think you can correct a child with and without spanking.

I know that there are a lot of people who might disagree with these verses as well. In today's society, we don't dare spank our children because it might damage their self-esteem. There are parents who just don't believe in it, and they are parenting a healthy, well-adjusted child.

I spanked my children, and I had family that didn't approve. I know their reasons, and I totally get it. I was abused as a child, and I was beat many times. And I can see how they would be afraid that history would repeat itself. I understand it is and can be a very touchy subject. I know my beliefs may not be yours, and I am okay with that. I won't treat anyone different because they don't believe in spanking. In my opinion, I believe that the verse speaks loud and clear. We are responsible for the way our children are raised. They need to be taught, like I said before. Please don't let me lose you because of this subject.

I feel like we have taken a few rabbit trails, maybe because I totally want to be done with this chapter. Every time I think I will end it, I am pushed to keep going. So I have to ask myself, what is it that I don't want to look at?

Well, duh, silly, the truth!

Remember when I said I wanted you to feel like it was just us, chilling with a cup of coffee or tea in the sunroom having a long chat? Well, this is where one of us has to get a refill or stretch our legs. And it is me.

It's been a few days since I sat here last. I had a very difficult time writing the things I did about my choices. My fear, I believe, comes from what others will think of my past, of my choices. A lot has happened in the last few days. Our college girl came home early for spring break! I'm so glad she did for many reasons, one being a very good childhood friend who she recently reconnected with died. This young lady was up against it all her life but was starting to make good choices. We watched her and our daughter grow up together, and it just breaks my heart she is gone. So our girl is just trying to process and walk through this, and as mom, I have to stand back and wait and let her know I am here for her. I can't control this one. So we pray.

I have always tried to shield our college girl from everything because of the way I was acting when her big sisters were little. I still made bad choices with her or didn't pay attention to things when I should have. Shielding her from handling her own feelings and emotions are not good either. It has made it harder I think on tough situations. I am so grateful she has the friends she does, and her faith in Jesus amazes me.

In these past few days, we also took our adopted son to teen challenge for anger issues and a few other issues. I can be thankful it is not just a place for addicts and alcoholics.

We are thankful that he has not touched that stuff at this point in his life. We have tried everything with and for him. He was diagnosed with RADS (reactive attachment disorder) when he was younger. Basically, it means his birth mother did not bond with him at all. So there is a big disconnect with attachments to others. Because it was his birth mother that caused this, it has been rough trying to have a relationship with him. There is no trust, and love is not understood very well. It's been a tough twelve years with him. There is some tough love going on with this kid, actually now he is eighteen. He has had a tough go from day one as well, and we just want to see him get it right.

I have always been tough on him, some out of instinct because of how he acted, some out of fear of who he would become if we didn't control his every move. That toughness has been good for him with structure, and he is not in jail, like a lot of kids with his diagnosis. Without that structure and my thumb on him, he had no self-control. He acts before he thinks on everything. I know that sometimes I was just not nice to him at all. Times I could care less how he felt after all I had been through with him. Even now, I like that he is not always here. I can breathe without being anxious or angry all the time. I pray that this works for him, that he makes it work.

I want to be able to be in the same room with him, laughing and playing board games like we have times before without him sabotaging it again, over and over again. I want him to be a productive adult and have healthy relationships, but most of all, I want him to have a relationship with Jesus.

As far as being a good stepmother, I wasn't always. Not that the kids were mean or disrespectful because they weren't. My stepson and I got along great. Bike rides every other weekend, joking around a lot. Then he noticed girls. I miss him. His kids and work keep him so busy.

I can't forget about my stepdaughter. Oh, that poor kid had such a tough time with me. She was and still is a daddy's girl. Actually, all the girls are daddy's girls. It has taken a long time for her and I to be where we are. She is a great mommy, and I am so proud of her. She is a blessing in our lives! She needs a giant medal for putting up with me as a stepparent!

As a foster parent to a total of thirty-one foster kids over a period of nine years, I totally blew it with some and did great with others. I messed up in a lot of ways with them. A few I was glad when the journey was over. There are those that I miss every single day. I didn't get on the right path with God until the last few kids were there. I went through the motions of church and praying at meal time. But that was it. So now, I have to seek forgiveness for leading some of these kids astray. One of them really doesn't want anything to do with me now because she couldn't handle the change of being a hypocrite to now, making my choices based on what God wants me to do. Not to mention, I wasn't there for some important moments for her. I don't think she realized I was trying to distance myself out of guilt, or just feeling like we no longer belonged. Maybe one day, we can sit and talk about it, and maybe she has moved forward with no desire to talk. I can only ask God what to do and ask for forgiveness with her too. From what I have seen, she is also a really good mommy to her little girls.

So you see, God allowed many kids in my life to guide, teach, love, and care for. And I did not always get it done the right way. I was not always a good mom. I have had to learn to like me, to love me, to know I am worthy because God loves me. I did not know that full truth back then. Without that knowledge, it made it easier to mess up. I was good at messing things up and messing up people's lives. I was angry, mean, yelled so much of the time. There were times we had fun and did things together, but I always reacted first. I always tried to or think I could control everything and everyone around me. I can't and could not.

As far as being a Grammy, I rock! I will love and hug and guide and teach and protect and speak and show my faith in Jesus without hesitation! That's what makes a good mom too. I have also learned I do all of that for my kids now too. I always hugged my kids and told them I love them. And I would go toe-to-toe with anyone when they messed with any of my kids. I forgot to learn some of the other important parenting responsibilities along the way like I mentioned before.

Now I am proud of the mom I have grown up to be. I thank God for that opportunity, to have that two hundred millionth chance to be better than before!

> Hear, O Israel; The Lord our God, the Lord is one. Love the Lord you God with all your heart and with all your soul and with all your strength. These commandments that I give you today are to be on your hearts. Impress them on your children. Talk about them when you sit at home

and when you walk along the road, when you lie down and when you get up. Tie them as symbols on your hands and bind them on your foreheads. Write them on the doorframes of your houses and on your gates. (Deuteronomy 6:4–9, NIV)

Responses

1. Showing her children what it means to love others without judging them.
2. Good question.
3. Someone who loves Jesus, your dad, and you, can't go wrong from there.
4. Putting your children before yourself.
5. Someone who understands.
6. A caring, loving, and nurturing person who stands by her children and supports them.
7. Someone who is always there even if she doesn't agree with you.
8. Love, compassion, and understanding. (2)
9. Faith, love, grace, mercy, and compassion as well as a healthy dose of crazy.
10. Unconditional love. (10)
11. Listen, care, no judgment, gentle guidance.
12. Being there for your child. Being parents first, then a friend, teaching them about God and Jesus. Teach rules, consequences, and rewards, questioning yourself a million times a day if you're a good mom.
13. Someone who is loving, tolerant, kind, and assertive.
14. Someone who is patient, kind, and forgiving.
15. Patience, kindness, rules! Being a good listener, teacher, sound guidance, and grace.
16. One that loves you unconditionally no matter what you do.
17. A person who loves Christ, teaches her children the way of the Lord. Listens to her children, is loving, kind, giving, nurturing, and not afraid to discipline.
18. I am not a good mom.
19. Love, a strong heart, a firm and tough love when needed.
20. Consistency.
21. The love of Christ!
22. Love.

23. One that provides discipline, gives her heart, and soul for your well-being and loves you unconditionally, even when you mess up.

24. Someone who is supportive, checks to make sure you are okay, allows you to make mistakes but is there to lend an ear, and who does not focus on material things but teaches good morals.

25. Love and patience.

26. Patience and hard work.

27. Someone who loves you, no matter what and is always in your corner. Someone who tells you when you are wrong but not in a way that puts you down; someone who teaches you things that she learned from her mother.

28. Love, truth from the Bible, and discipline.

29. Taking time to listen to your children.

30. Patience. (2)

31. Love and compassion.

32. Loving your kids and doing the best you can for them.

33. A woman that tries, cares, shows love and doesn't withhold it even if she's mad at you.

34. Someone who realizes a child is a gift from God and not a possession they get to control.

35. Time and unconditional love.

36. Unconditional love and a listening ear.

37. Love, compassion, forgiveness and honesty.

38. Patience and a teaching heart.

39. Trying your best and keep trying.

40. Love, compassion, understanding, trust and faith.

41. Loving your family.

42. Loving, supportive, believes in you and encourages.

43. Someone who sticks by her kids no matter what.

44. Someone who gives moral and emotional support, someone who loves and accepts you for who you are.

45. Someone who is there for their children believes in them and never leaves.

46. A good mom is someone who loves and cares for their children unconditionally. Teaching them life skills so they could be independent and also teaching them how to be a "good" person.
47. Love, honesty, and nurturing.
48. Someone who takes care of you, is tough on you, and teaches you things that you need to know.
49. Making sure their child is happy.
50. Consistency and steadfastness.
51. Showing up.
52. Guidance, understanding, and love.
53. Doing the best you can. Not trying to be perfect, teaching your children about our heavenly Father, instilling manners and rules.
54. Once beat my child, I always sought corroboration before any punishment.
55. Look up my mother LOL! You know the old saying? Anyone can have a baby? That's not true. So, how about this, a mother does not always have biological children. A mother is kind, soft, big-hearted, but at the same, time will put a boot up your hind end when you need it (speaking from experience ha-ha). You put your children's wants and needs above yourself always! One day, these children will grow up and move out, then what? You can try your hardest to guide them through life and raise them to be a positive part of society and good hard working adults and eventually mothers themselves. A real mother will always be with you through the good and bad.
56. Knowing Jesus.
57. Love, patience, determination.
58. Attention and unconditional love.
59. Caring, nurturing, always positive vibes.
60. Love, attention and understanding.
61. Love, compassion, guidance and rules.
62. Big hearts and big ears.
63. Knowing Christ first.

64. Always being there for us and setting a good example, a loving, compassionate, empathetic, and gracious soul.
65. Patience, understanding, tenacity, God, ability to set standards and follow through them and wisdom.
66. A mother that loves the Lord and loves her kids.
67. Time spent, grace and kind heart.
68. Love, kindness, respect and honesty.
69. Honesty.
70. Nurture, discipline, and laughter.
71. Love, patience, kindness, gentleness, and *self*-control.
72. Love and a looot of patience with some good communication and listening skills.
73. Love, resilience, and trying.
74. Love and support, no matter what. Even when kids do something wrong, they need discipline, but they also need to know that they are still loved. How God is loving and forgiving of us is the example.
75. Someone who would stop at nothing to keep their children safe. Even if it meant saying no to something they wanted that might not be good for them. Someone who doesn't doubt their children but encourages them rather than breaking them down with doubt.
76. Love, respect, and dedication.
77. A kind, compassionate, loving heart, love, hugs, smiles, and the ability to correct.
78. Love, listening, and support even if you don't always agree! Let them make choices and mistakes to learn from them!
79. Spend as much time with them *as I can.*
80. One who teaches the love of Christ, is warm and affectionate, offers life lessons and instructions.
81. Jesus and true love.
82. Gentleness, caring, listening, and love.
83. Unconditional love, compassion, fairness, a love for God. To know, understand, and receive God's love and forgiveness helps me to give that to my children.

84. Always being there for your children regardless of how you feel about what they are doing, even if you don't agree. Never make them feel as though you aren't there for them.
85. A woman of God, who would sacrifice and do whatever she could to make you happy, feel loved, wanted, and needed.
86. A mom who walks really close to God and teaches her children the same as my mom did.
87. Patience, love, kindness, understanding, discipline, prayers, faith, constant conversations, and engaged in your child's life and what's going on.
88. A good listener, loving, kind, soft-spoken, and knowing when you are hurting and knowing what to say and do. Being the Jesus kind of example of love and acceptance, kind smile, soft touch, best friend, good hugger, and being able to set boundaries.
89. Someone who supports you with whatever you decide to do in life. Cares about you and understands you, helps you when you're hurt or down, talks to you about anything. Is there for you no matter what and will do anything for you when needed.
90. Love and discipline and putting Jesus into your life!
91. I can't be a judge of that. I talk a big game, but I don't really know about motherhood—and I won't until I reach that stage of life. Love and patience are huge components, but it takes so much more than that. There is so much pressure to be a good mom; I don't think there is any right way to be a good mom.
92. Loving, nonjudgmental, she has open arms.

Now it's your turn to answer.

What makes a good mom?

_____
_____
_____
_____
_____
_____
_____
_____
_____
_____
_____
_____
_____
_____
_____
_____
_____
_____
_____
_____
_____
_____
_____
_____
_____
_____
_____
_____
_____
_____

Chapter 19

What Would You Pass On to Your Child That Would Tell Them How Much You Love Them?

I actually thought about leaving this question out of the book. Even now, I'm sure my kids know I love them. But what if I couldn't say the words *I love you*? How else would they know? What if I could only pass on one thing that would give them the best chance at a healthy spiritual life?

The one thing I can say that speaks of love, discipline, trust, faith, relationships, and how to walk in this dark world is the Word of God, the Bible. Yes, it would be the Bible. There are so many life experiences in this book that imitate today's world. There are so many examples of how to get through the troubles and the struggles in life. There are moments of being angry and running and trying to hide from God. Times when He says He sees you. He speaks to the little ones and the older generations. He fights for you and calls others to fight for what is right, and He equips them to do so. When people didn't listen, he punished them as He even holds us accountable today. There are warnings about doing bad or going against Him, just like a good Father, He lets us know what He wants from us. There are also rewards for doing what is right for our brothers and sisters. There is sacrifice and pain; there is unconditional love. It's about a mighty battle of good versus evil, and good wins! There is temptation and how to overcome it. It's about a baby born to grow and teach and save us from ourselves. It's about healing and walking the right path. It's about forgiveness and salvation, eternity in peace or eternity in pain. It's everything you need.

There are so many lessons in the Bible that need to be taught and learned and passed on. So many lessons that I failed to teach or learn. So as I learn, I try and lead and teach what I have learned. I know it will take a lifetime to learn all that has been laid out in the pages of my Bible. My regret is that I didn't start sooner. My joy is I'm not giving up! Something I have learned through this journey of being a Christian, a believer, a person who has a relationship with Jesus, is that fellowship with other believers is important. I need that time with other people to spur me on in my walk. That way, if my walk starts to sway too far, one way or the other off the path, I have brothers and sisters to guide me back.

When I get it right, they are also there to celebrate with me as well. I don't understand everything I read in the Bible, but that is also why fellowship is important. There are sixty-six books in the Bible with so much information that to try and chew it up by yourself would be so difficult. That is another reason I believe in meeting with other believers.

So if I had to choose one way to show my children how much I love them and I could only give one thing, I would hand them my Bible.

Old Testament

Genesis, Exodus, Leviticus, Numbers, Deuteronomy, Joshua, Judges, Ruth, 1 Samuel, 2 Samuel, 1 Kings, 2 Kings, 1 Chronicles, 2 Chronicles, Ezra, Nehemiah, Esther, Job, Psalms, Proverbs, Ecclesiastes, Song of Songs, Isaiah, Jeremiah, Lamentations, Ezekiel, Daniel, Hosea, Joel, Amos, Obadiah, Jonah, Micah, Nahum, Habakkuk, Zephaniah, Haggai, Zechariah, Malachi

New Testament

Matthew, Mark, Luke, John, Acts, Romans, 1 Corinthians, 2 Corinthians, Galatians, Ephesians, Philippians, Colossians, 1

Thessalonians, 2 Thessalonians, 1 Timothy, 2 Timothy, Titus, Philemon, Hebrews, James, 1 Peter, 2 Peter, 1 John, 2 John, 3 John, Jude, Revelation

I would encourage them to seek answers, and if I don't know them, I would try and direct them to the answer or person who would know better than I. But because there is no limit of what I would pass on, then I would have to say living skills.

Budgeting money is so important, and I wish I would have learned much sooner how to do this. I came from nothing, and we didn't have much growing up. Growing up, it was sometimes about the things we didn't have, and as a mom, I found I wanted to give my kids everything I did not have as a kid. That's not a good idea either, but I tried. So I spent a lot of money on stuff. My husband had a great job that provided for everything we needed and some things we really wanted. But I thought if I had checks then I had money. I bounced many checks before we talked about what I was doing. Money was not something that my parents talked about because they never had much of it. The foster families didn't really talk about money, and when I was married the first time, I knew we didn't have a lot of money. We would go to the grocery store, and after things were rung up, I would have the cashier take things off the bill. The last time that happened with him, I left the cart where it was and walked out. When we got home, I made him sell three guns so I could go back and do grocery shopping with no worries. I didn't go over well until I called his father. Do what you have to, I guess.

When I was on cash assistance if I didn't have enough money for diapers or drugs, I used what I had to get it myself. When I got married again, and like I said, my hubby had a great job. I didn't know how to handle having money. I didn't have to degrade myself or cause myself more shame, and I didn't have to sell belongings either. So money is so important to talk about.

Cooking, we have to eat, and no, I do not always eat healthy. Actually, I don't even have to cook that much because my husband loves to cook. Since he retired from the PSP, he cooks all the time. Lately, we have been working in the kitchen together, and I really enjoy that time with him. I love working in the kitchen with the kids too. This Thanksgiving or Christmas, I want to teach the girls how to make homemade biscotti! You know what is really just a great feeling? It's when you make a dish that the family loves, lasagna, and your girl calls and asks how you make yours! I love that she tweaked it even to suit her kids. That is so awesome to me. I'm waiting for them to have recipes that I get to borrow. Actually, that has happened with my stepdaughter.

I enjoy gardening and working in the flower beds. The girls used to help me in the garden and flower beds when we lived in Huntingdon. When the tomato plants would get really tall, I could sit in the garden and hide from them. LOL.

Then they just started looking there first when the garden was growing well. Since we moved to this town almost seven years ago, we haven't really done a lot of gardening. And even when we did, the girls are growing up with things to do and other responsibilities. Panda did have time between breaks to help plant a few new flowers last year before my knee surgery. As the flowers grew, I would send pictures of the progress and because calla lilies are one of her favorites. So this summer, since my knee is much better, I will get to finish making the one flower bed bigger and maybe get a little help. Hint, hint!

Plus, I think Bratsy wants to plant a few flowers at her new place this summer, and she asked me to help. I can't wait!

So what else is there? They know how to clean a house, although that was tough for them to learn because I was such a control freak. Everything had to be done my way or don't bother, from dishes to the towels folded a certain way. I think what I want them to learn is let their kids learn in the best way for them. If they are trying to help you and you want it done a certain way, teach. Let them try, a few times if they must. But don't redo it when they walk away; they will see you have done it, and it will crush them! I wish I had paid attention sooner to what I was doing. I used to change the way they folded their own clothes. I wasn't allowing them to learn or try. I was stifling their learning abilities, their independence. I was projecting my OCD on to them. I hope you don't teach your children that way, girls, it wasn't fair to you when I did it.

I know that Christmas has been my holiday for a long time. It is where I feel the most joy, and I hope they start traditions like I have as they have their own homes and families. I don't think any of the kids want the 280 buildings or all the accessories that go with the Christmas villages that get put up every year!

I hope that they have learned how to have fun, to laugh, and not hold back. To make joy and laughter happen even if that means they ambush their kids or each other with nerf guns. We have four; they can totally borrow them! Sometimes, you just have to sit with a bowl of your favorite ice cream and watch a comedy until you cry when your day has been tough. Sometimes, it's grabbing the tennis racquet and rocking out, cranking the music up, and dancing like crazy. It's water fights with the hose, yes, sometimes it happens in the house! I wonder if the kids remember the mud pit in October we made at the old house! That was cold and a blast! Bottom line, it's about being able to laugh and smile.

The kids are already smart, and I am proud of all of them. But there is something that book smarts can't teach, and that is street smarts. What I mean by that is just teaching them to be aware of their surroundings. Not to have their faces in the electronics all of the time, to be alert, prepared not paranoid. John, Panda, and I went to New York one year around Christmas time; it was absolutely beautiful with all the lights but extremely busy with people constantly. Panda was on her phone and walking ahead of us. Her dad and I were watching a guy start walking up closer to her. And then his pace was a bit faster, and he was way too close to make this mom happy. So I yelled to her to wait up, and the guy looked back at me. I watched his face as he realized we were getting closer to him as he got closer to our daughter. He backed off so fast; I still wanted to tackle him just for trying to get near her in an unhealthy way. We were pretty sure he was looking at her purse. But because we were alert, it turned out good for her. That's what I want for the kids. I want them to pay attention to what is happening around them because you never know who it will protect.

I have always been honest about my past and drug abuse. Not tons of detail, unless they ask. But they do know the story of how their dad and I met. And no, I was not acting the best I could have; I was in active addiction and being totally stupid. My purpose for telling them was simple. With my family history of drugs and alcohol and my being an addict and alcoholic, they need to know their chances are increased of being the same if they use even once. If they choose to drink, that is on them and I don't get mad at them for it. They have the information they need to make the best choices. If I see they begin to have a problem, they know I will talk to them about it. That leads me to the last thing I would want them to have. I want them to have the kind of relationship we have now with their kids. The kind that says you can talk to me about anything anytime. No matter what it is or the reaction they think will come out. I know there are things they don't share with me, and that is okay too. When it counts, they know I am there. That's what I want for all of them as their kids grow up and begin to find their way in life.

Even when I am old and weak, fragile and slow, I pray they still come to me to talk, to laugh, to cry and just sit with me, to ask for advice and share their life stories with me. To still let me be Mom, and them my wonderful children.

Responses

1. What it means to love others without judging them.
2. Unconditional love. (4)
3. Give them time and literally tell them you love them.
4. Verbal affirmation every day that I love her.
5. Understanding.
6. I always show my children unconditional love and support.
7. Reach for the stars and never give up. Spending time with them, making them feel heard and special.
8. Affection and compassion.
9. A legacy of faith in Christ Jesus as well as a firm foundation.
10. Memories. (3)
11. Listen, care, no judgment, and gentle guidance.
12. Traditions of family.
13. That no matter what happens in life, I am their family, and I will always be here for them.
14. My kind heart and honesty.
15. I have tried to pass on the fact that I'm always there for them if they want or need my help, they need only ask.
16. My cross necklace.
17. To always tell them you love them. (4)
18. Simply the way I treat them.
19. My love for them and any advice I could give them.
20. A letter stating it.
21. Warm embracing hugs and kisses on the forehead! God's Word!
22. I show them in all that I do and all that I am.
23. The ability to teach them forgiveness, love, and kindness to others.
24. Being a support and modeling how to be a good person.
25. Their handmade baby hats and blankets.
26. Quality time. (1)
27. I would be there for them, to listen, give advice, and cheer on.
28. That Jesus loves them.

29. I will be there for them no matter what. (2)
30. Lots of actions of love and quality time.
31. Outings. I love going on trips with family and friends. Put away technology and just go somewhere to enjoy nature, art, and each other.
32. Time and unconditional love.
33. Love, compassion, forgiveness, and honesty.
34. You can do anything you set your mind to.
35. Be involved in their loves and always be an example of Jesus Christ.
36. Love, acceptance, and faith.
37. Advice and memories.
38. Jesus, I would want to make sure they know Him.(2)
39. Not to do the things I did and not things my mom did.
40. Time spent with them making memories. (2)
41. Show how much they are loved and wanted.
42. Just being there for them. (2)
43. I constantly let my children know I love them for who they are, and that they're okay to make mistakes but to learn from their mistakes.
44. I love you.
45. Each night, I write into different journals for each child, telling them about our day and life.
46. I think how much I love them is by my action. I tell my children every day that I love them, but it's everything I also do for them so they feel my love.
47. Being kind.
48. My wisdom and experience.
49. I take time for each of my kids to have me-time every day, and once a month, I spend time with each kid one on one.
50. A letter.
51. Hugs. (2)
52. Actions speak louder than words.
53. Teach and show your children how to become productive, acceptable adults by example. Praise them when they

deserve it. Say the words "I love you" often! Caring and love go hand-in-hand.

54. You can never make me not love you, no matter what you do. Learn from your mistakes and move on. If you think you are alone, just look around.
55. My poems.
56. Everything my mom taught me.
57. A heart of kindness.
58. Stick to what you know is right.
59. My understanding of nonjudgment, verbal and physical acts of love. Hugs and words of encouragement.
60. I try to pass on my faith that God is faithful and powerful.
61. Stories.
62. Belief in them.
63. A book from my perspective about our relationship.
64. How much strength they have within them.
65. The fact that I believe in them and anything they would try to do.
66. My actions.
67. Memories of quality-time spent together.
68. Love, honesty, and respect.
69. Good advice.
70. I would read to them every night until they get to big. Then I would buy them books that I would love for them to read.
71. My time and telling them how much I love and care about them.
72. Always here if you need me! No matter good or bad!
73. Spend as much time with them as I can.
74. Stay strong in your faith in Christ as Savior. Eternal things are more important than temporal tangible things. We are never alone; God is always with us and we can count on Him even when those we love have gone on. I love you with everything in me.
75. Be there and show love.
76. Strength.

77. Showing that I love them and leaving absolutely no doubt that I do indeed love them. That's my legacy to them.
78. I have journals for my daughter.
79. That she is beautiful in the eyes of the Lord and in my eyes. And that I will be there for her no matter what!
80. To love Jesus with every ounce of their heart.
81. My love for the Lord. It brings all the happiness in the world, and I want them to be happy and to always be able to make the right decisions.
82. Love, love, love and daily hugs, question how they are, and how their day was. Be interested in them sincerely.
83. Be kind to everyone and treat people the way you want to be treated. Always respect your mother, no matter what. You only get one mom in your life, and when she's gone, she's gone. One day, you will need her when you think you won't. In the end, she will always love you and care about you even if she doesn't show it or say it. You may have mom figures in your life, but none will be the same as your real mom.
84. Pass on a love for and a following of Jesus!
85. I would pass on my great-grandmothers Christmas ornaments.
86. Writing to them. While I'm away from home, my mom writes notes to me on cards. Usually just whatever is on her heart—her hopes and prayers for me, encouragement, and thoughts in general. It may seem like a small gesture to others, but they mean a lot to me. They are usually filled with hard or heartfelt truths. They are deeply genuine.

Now it's your turn to answer.

What would you pass on to your child that would tell them how much you love them?

_____

_____

_____

_____

_____

_____

_____

_____

_____

_____

_____

_____

_____

_____

_____

_____

_____

_____

_____

_____

_____

_____

_____

_____

Chapter 20

If You Know There Are Missing Mom Pieces in Your Heart, Do You Know What They Are?

Missing Mom pieces, what does that even mean? When I wrote out these questions, the one thought I had was that it always seems like I am missing out on something. And then it was like, duh, you have missed out on having your mother in your life and all the things and events mothers should be there for. Or at least want to be there for. So it could be anything from not having her around during your childhood, missing the birth of your own children, a bad relationship in general. I can't decide what that is for you. I hope that you have no missing pieces. But the completed questionnaires I received say differently.

I have spent years, okay, forever trying my best to keep all of this locked up inside of my own heart and mind. If I didn't look at it as a hurtful thing, then I could just keep it as if I am just mad a lot. Growing up, we were not allowed to show emotion such as anger, pain, or even disappointment. Even getting scolded or hit as a kid, you were not allowed to cry or we heard "keep crying and I will give you something to cry about."

Now fear, oh, that better be seen because our house was run on fear. If we were afraid or coward when a hand was raised at us, my father was doing it all right. He prided himself on being that way with the kids, my mother, and anyone that would not or could not stand up to him. So I believe that leads me into some of my first missing pieces. She didn't fight for me; she didn't take us and run and never go back. I'm not looking for stats about how many times it takes to leave an abusive relationship; I totally know about that through living it as a child and an adult. The fact that there are stats on this are so sad because that means there are enough cases someone needs to put a percentage on our actions or nonactions. The stats prove there is a problem, and the problem is domestic abuse. And if our eyes are open to numbers, then we know that behind the numbers are faces of women and men and children being beaten; ignored; verbally, emotionally, and mentally beat down over and over again. Day after day, bruises are being explained away with excuses of how accidents happen, or they were promised it would never happen again, and they were really sorry this time. So every other apology was a lie? Do you know we put our abuse on a scale most times, without realizing it? Okay, so he slapped me, but if he puts his hands on my throat, I'm gone, or if he closes his hand next time or does it again. We do not value our own lives as we should. Or what about I can handle it, but if he goes for my kid, then I'm gone? If you have those thoughts, leave now. Because that means you know the kid could be next. You know that is a fear you have, and it will probably happen. There is something else to think about, not guilty you, but to really think about. What if he hurts you so bad, or kills you, who will raise your child? Who will protect them if you are gone? If you are hurting, I am hurting with you, for you.

National Domestic Violence Hotline:
 # 1-800-799-SAFE (7233)

I used to feel guilty for being angry at her because she always hurt too. But I want to stand up and stomp up and down and scream how bad I hurt. I want to be able to just let it all out and never look at it again. I want to take all of the things that she said or did and form it into the biggest dodge ball and blast her with it. It hurts when someone turns their back on you, even more when it is the woman who helped you come into this world and should love you.

One of my pieces is how in the world could she marry my father after what he did to her? They were not married the night I was conceived. Knowing the pain that caused, how could she do it? I feel like she set us all up for even more of a horrible life by marrying him. She didn't need a baby daddy that bad, or did she? I was number four after all. I understand how that statement sounds. I have given birth to three daughters who all have different biological fathers. I didn't need baby daddies; I just wanted someone to want me for me.

Some of my pieces are how my siblings were treated. She knew about the abuse the kids suffered, and yet again, she did nothing. I cannot speak for any of the other kids, but it makes me angry we spent a lifetime apart because she couldn't and wouldn't get her life together. It would be twenty-one years after I was taken away for the last time that four out of five kids would be together.

"But I will sing of your strength, in the morning I will sing of your love; for you are my fortress, my refuge in times of trouble. You are my strength, I sing praise to you; you, God, are my fortress, my God on whom I can rely" (Psalm 59:16–17, NIV).

October 24, 2014, I flew to Oregon. This is what I felt the need to share as I waited for their arrival. In the early morning hours, before the light peaks up and says hello to the world, at least the west coast, you realize all these years what you wanted you are about to get. You realize that fear kept you cold so you don't have to feel. And you realize even more that the pain you feel is not totally horrible memories but of missing out!

Missing simple gestures as a hug or smile on a daily, weekly basis, you missed birthdays and holidays. And you blame anyone of "the other four." When in all reality, they probably feel the same way! You can't really lash out at the ones responsible because they are gone or not well enough to care. There is no justice to be found here. And in those moments you share your deepest thoughts, you realize there is nothing to fear. God has been preparing me all these twenty-one years for this day, this day to see, forgive, and remember! This day where I, we, can share hugs, smiles, laughter, and probably tears. And that's okay. I am a child of God, and today He teaches me!

"So do not fear, for I am with you; do not be dismayed, for I am your God. I will strengthen you and help you; I will uphold you with my righteous right hand" (Isaiah 41:10, NIV).

It was a great visit, reunion. I think it was harder for some to stay in contact since then. There was so much guilt and anger and sadness that wasn't addressed for a few. I had hoped that we would continue to grow together and get to know each other again. What I found in the last four years of that reunion is that there is still a distance for a few. I am learning to take care of myself in all areas, and I made a choice to protect myself. I was becoming unhealthy within the desire to work so hard at having a severely strained relationship with biological family members.

I would want to send you a message when I saw your face pop up in my social media. Fear and anxiety would take over instead of a smile at the thought of us talking. Fear of rejection that I have felt for years when I needed you. Too many times of you just ignoring that I was there or a quick hi and love you. I want a relationship with family that I don't have to work or care more about than you do. If I do all of it on my own, I might as well talk to myself. I wanted to be here for you in your success and mishaps, in your celebrations and struggles. Also the other way around, I want to talk to you when life is going great and talk about my dreams or if I had a bad day. I need to be able to share with you too, not feel like it is a bother for you to listen.

I know I am in a different place than you; I'm not better than you, just in a different place. And that's okay. What's not okay is it seems we can't admit this is not working. Maybe concern that the others can't handle it. We have to be healthy no matter what side we are on. I can't be if it is too difficult for you to have a relationship with me. I will always question whether you are really there completely or just going through the motions out of guilt. It's not your guilt to own anymore. I will still answer if you call because I want to know you; I want you to be in my life. When you are ready, I am here. I know we won't have it all together; I just want there to be a real desire to be family, to move the pain aside, and go down the next road together.

Why did I say all of that? It is the ripple effect of how being a bad parent plays out as your kids get older. It is part of the missing pieces.

Now on to the next missing piece of my puzzle, she didn't teach me how to be a mom. She taught me what not to do, and I still acted like her sometimes that makes me want to throw the whole family puzzle out the window. Because that's what we were, a giant family puzzle, with each person having an important place to fit. And some of the pieces are missing; some are ripped, and maybe some just fell through the cracks of life. But we are not whole or glued together, instead we are tattered and mangled with pain, fear, and denial. My pieces went deeper than I thought they did. I really just thought I could skate through this cool idea for a book and help others maybe get closer to God and some answer God when he called their names and help some to not hurt so bad anymore because there were others who understood a little bit of their pain.

As I sit here and my husband is at the main computer, I fight to hold tears and frustration and sadness in. I don't want him to see this is difficult or weakening me.

"Three times I pleaded with the Lord to take it away from me. But he said to me, 'My grace is sufficient for you, for my power is made perfect in weakness.' Therefore I will boast all the more gladly about my weaknesses, so that Christ's power may rest on me" (2 Corinthians 13:8–9, NIV).

My biggest two pieces about my mom is she abandoned me and she didn't protect me from the monster in the house or show me how to avoid future monsters in my life.

I am angry! I am hurting! I am sad at the loss I feel! All of these years I have been going through the grieving process and never realized it until now! I have always been that adult child waiting for the phone to ring with approval from my mother.

The phone is never going to ring, and she will never know me well enough to know what I need. I will never have her approval because she doesn't care what I do or where I am in my life. She will not know I cry for her when life just stinks sometimes, or when I really want to call and ask for advice about a marriage question.

What about the silly questions about cooking? I can't ask about that either.

Sometimes, I just want to hear her voice and know that she is just as happy about hearing mine. Sometimes, I just want a phone call from her just to hear her say she loves me, without me saying it first, and then she says she loves me because she feels it's something she is being forced to do. She has never done that. She has my number, and I have hers. But she doesn't care how my day went yesterday, today, or tomorrow. I can imagine I sound like I am being a baby, but what it really is, is me admitting for the first time that this is how she is and always has been.

She doesn't ask about the grandchildren or the great-grandchildren. She has no idea how many there are; she doesn't want to know. Or she would call; she would ask.

I wonder if she has avoided me because of how I was, as in the addiction part of my life. Actually, that is just giving her too much credit because she knew that I did drugs and drank. We never have really had the chance to talk about it. She changed the subject the few times I brought it up. What I wanted to tell her is I don't blame her for my choice to drink and be a drug addict. Just because I grew up around it didn't mean I had to choose it for myself. I wanted to confide in her about the depression and ask questions. I wanted to know if when she went into the hospital for a nervous breakdown, did she try to kill herself too? And if so, was it only once or multiple times too? Did she overdose before and ever get mad when having her stomach pumped worked? Did she dream of dying and then wonder who would actually miss her? Did she eat whatever pills she could find to just sleep forever and ever? Did she drive too fast, act careless, and anger people so they would put her out of her misery? I did those things, Mom. So many times I wanted to close my eyes and never open them again. I just wanted to die, be dead, not breath ever again. I wanted death over pain. I wanted death over life. I wanted to die.

Was she angry when she realized it didn't work the way she wanted? I wanted to ask her how she got through it because I never saw her take medication. I do, and I just wanted to know if that was okay with her. Did it make me look weak because I couldn't handle the pain in my life, and I was afraid to reach out. I was afraid no one would grab my hand back. I just wanted to talk to my mom and tell her I am okay now.

I just wanted the hurt I felt to leave me, and I never understood there was another way, until I met Jesus. He came into my heart and warmed it and filled it with love that I had never known before. I didn't want to die anymore. Instead, I want to help others live. Have you experienced that, Mom?

National Suicide Hotline # 1-800-273-TALK (8255)

I have spent my life trying to force a relationship with her that she didn't want. And in the end, I am the one that became or stayed unhealthy. It's like trying to fit a jumbo-floor-size puzzle piece into a five-hundred-piece puzzle when the pieces are an inch big. It doesn't work on either side.

Maybe I sound like a spoiled brat who never gave her a chance. I wish I was a spoiled brat that was just mad because my mom spent five minutes more on the phone with a sibling than me. If that was the case, we would not be here right now.

Even after all of this, admitting my messed up pieces of pain and sadness I feel guilty. I think the guilt is easier than anger. I think for me anger keeps her away more on my part. What I mean by that is when I am angry, I don't keep trying to force a mother-daughter relationship. I don't get depressed, but I stay tense and teeth-clenched and a bit standoffish. That is what I considered healthy for so long. And then, it is in black and white, and I realize how foolish that all looks.

So there you have it, my missing Mom pieces are out. Now I have to figure out how to deal with them and be healthy. Not my kind of past healthy but healthy in God.

Responses

1. They have been healed.
2. Yes there are MMPs for sure. Love being the easiest to recognize.
3. There is a missing piece for where my babies would have grown. (I had miscarriages) and also wish that I had done better for the child God gave me (a foster son).
4. I think I was too hard on my daughter for somethings. I thought she had to be perfect. (Christy, I am transcribing this for Mom. She was never too hard on me. —Sheila).
   a) *I believe all moms desire to hear this from their adult children!* Thank you, Sheila, for your daughter's heart toward your mom!
5. Yes. (6)
6. Missing my mom.
7. A mother's love and gentleness.
8. The part of my mom that trusts me enough to discuss feelings and apprehensions. I miss my mom a lot. I'm not an earthly mom; I have a child in heaven, so not having my child with me too.
9. Having an older mom, I miss doing things that younger mom do with their daughters.
10. No, not anymore. (2)
11. Unconditional love.
12. No/Nah/none here. (10)
13. I think I was always resented; she was so confrontational.
14. I wish she would have told me she loved me except for the day before she died.
15. I know there are missing pieces just not what they are.
16. Hugs and kisses.
17. I cannot remember her hugging me or giving me a kiss!
18. She was always too busy working.
19. My mom worked full time and sometimes worked at night, so she didn't always get to come to things at school. I wish she would have come to more.

20. Her absence.
21. No idea.
22. Started off at twenty with no memories, had to learn to be a daughter and a mother at the same time.
23. I don't know exactly what they, are but they hurt.
24. Forgiveness.
25. I have the mom that God gave me. I wish she valued our relationship more, but I love her and wouldn't want another mom.
26. Unsure.
27. She didn't encourage me enough, and she didn't really believe in me like she should've.
28. When my child passed away at twenty-weeks pregnant.
29. Just the loss of her and I wasn't there.
30. Yes, my mom is no longer in my life as a mom. She feels like a mostly distant aunt or cousin I see a few times a year.
31. Yes, abandonment. (3)
32. There are so many things I miss about my mom. I miss my mom's cooking, her sewing skills, her generosity, and so much more.
33. We don't spend as much time together as I would like.
34. I am not sure. I know I need to forgive her, but I have always struggled to.
35. My actual mom.
36. Would have loved a closer relationship with my mother. She had no idea how my ex-husband treated me because she never came around when I moved from home.
37. I wish my bio mom loved me as much as my foster mom did.
38. There are none of her pieces; her pieces are and were not allowed! Good or bad because I was repulsed by her way of mothering!
39. I still have guilt about missing two years of my kids' lives when they were younger. I turned to alcohol and drugs to stay sane, but in reality, they made me crazy. But I proceeded and took the steps I needed to get help and learn

and grow and have my kids back. And the two children I lost to early miscarriages to abusive partners in the past still ache at my heart. I cry for the unborn but know God knew what was best, and I agree. He allowed me to have two more beautiful, healthy, happy children that I very much enjoy now.

40. Not telling or showing how much I loved and appreciated her.
41. She's bipolar and has been untreated and in denial her whole life and has made family suffer.
42. Her here.
43. The missing pieces in my heart are not there because of my mom, if anything, she helped them not be as big.
44. A sense that my mom is proud of me, that she loves me unconditionally.
45. Time with her, she died at age sixty-one.
46. Willingness to do things even though she doesn't like it.
47. Listening and understanding my feelings and needs.
48. Fun or joy and adventure. I can have a deep conversation about life and hurt, hope, but we rarely laugh together. She's hurting on the inside, and I really do not think that she sees the fun anymore. She used to be spontaneous when I was little, and now she questions every decision or weekend plan.
49. The confidence to know I am raising my children right, the confidence to push myself to be a better person. All the things I was never shown or taught with my own mother.
50. It would be easier to inventory the existing pieces.
51. It's tough being a new parent, parenting without your own mother.
52. Her presence. She passed at fifty-nine when I was twenty-seven. I miss her terribly.
53. Too many, not sure.
54. My mom as a whole, I miss her love.
55. I wish I felt that unconditional love. I wish I never doubted or questioned whether or not she loved me.

56. Acceptance, tolerance, and understanding.
57. I feel like there are a lot. Because of my choices and the way my mom felt about those choices, she missed a lot of important moments. The biggest pieces are the birth of my children. I hate those are the memories she is missing from.
58. I think her and I as Christians have become closer through Christ. We are good with each other.
59. Most of them questions, answers, guidance.
60. I wish my mother would have been stricter on me when I was growing up.
61. Not really, but I could never do to my children what my mom has put me through.
62. Rejection, acceptance, needing discipline, learning how to set healthy boundaries. She has never accepted my kids fully or wants to spend time with them.
63. She has a lot of health problems that I wish I can just fix for her so she is not in pain. I want to help her with more things. I also want to understand why she does some of the things she does.
64. I miss her love, conversations, and visits now that she's in heaven.
65. Hurt, angry, and alone.
66. Wanting her to be less judgmental.
67. Not being able to be there all the time.

Now it's your turn.

If you know there are missing Mom pieces in your heart, do you know what they are?

_____

_____

_____

_____

_____

_____

_____

_____

_____

_____

_____

_____

_____

_____

_____

_____

_____

_____

_____

_____

_____

_____

_____

_____

_____

_____

_____

Chapter 21

How Has God Healed You from Those Missing Pieces?

God is still working on me to heal. I have to call out to Him because He won't force healing on me. He won't force me to come to Him and say, "Lord, please heal me." This question is one of the biggest reasons for writing this.

Healing for me begins with being in the Word daily. I will admit there are days I don't get in the Bible, and when that happens, those days can be pretty rough. If I miss the family gathering on Sundays (church), then the rest of the week is difficult. I find that some mornings are despised, and I don't want to get out of bed. I could easily stay in bed until noon if I had nothing planned. And as soon as I planned or agreed to do something, I started having thoughts of canceling due to anxiety. Rainy days do not help, so I remind myself that God uses the rain to make flowers grow, and I love flowers. God gifted people with the ability to come up with medications for depression and the issues that can come with that. So I became proactive and got back on it. I had a difficult time with trying to figure out if it was right for me. Did I not trust God enough to take the depression, the OCD, or the PTSD? Was I not fighting hard enough to be okay? Was I fighting depression and the other issues because of sin in my life? The answer to that is no!

I needed meds for depression, and it was no different than having a heart issue or a sugar issue. So you might think if people with heart or sugar issues don't take meds, they could die. And that is

219

correct. So how does that compare to me feeling as if I need meds? When I am not on them, I do not always make the best choices. Even getting up to take a shower or wash my hair becomes a huge struggle, and sometimes, it just didn't happen. Not taking meds makes it easier to choose to drink again or use again, and that is not an option that is best for me or my family.

There was a time I did not take my med, and I was drinking and drugging. The things I did put me in the psyche unit for a week. My poor husband had to turn his back and walk away, leaving me there angry and scared. I can't imagine how he felt when I went from scared and nervous and telling him I was okay to screaming I hated him for walking away. Even though it was the best thing for me, for us. The things I put him and our children through all because I couldn't face my problems. He even put his badge and gun on the table with the higher ups because they told him he needed to be there for a meeting. He was willing to walk away from his job in that moment or face discipline to help me get the help I needed.

There is way too much stigma on mental health issues. It makes it harder when there are people who think you are dealing with mental illness because of a sin. I'm not saying every Christian thinks that. I thought for a long time my sin must have caused it for God not to take it from me. It is hard trying to figure out mental health issues and the emotions that come with it. I have had to learn how to stand up for myself and speak out when things get tough. Not blame everything on my depression, but if I am hurting or struggling then say something. How you do things to others is just as important.

"Let your conversation be always full of grace, seasoned with salt, so that you may know how to answer everyone" (Colossians 4:6, NIV).

I find that verse difficult sometimes when my emotions have taken over. I want to learn how to be that person that speaks love and compassion first, no matter what the situation. I haven't always done this, especially when it comes to my mother.

I care for my mom from a distance and with no expectations. Part of that is because I have a hard time being kind and compassionate with her. I am much healthier when there is no contact. I know that I said I want that, but it has never been healthy. I have told myself over and over again that I can make this relationship happen, and it will all be okay. That is called wanting what I know I can't have. If she can't take responsibility for her part, then she is not healthy enough for a relationship with me. I can't trust she will be in the right frame of mind to be honest with me about anything. For years, it has been an out-of-sight out-of-mind relationship on her side. My side is how do I fix it, her? I have been willing to deal with the pain and roller coaster ride just to say I have a mom in my life. Even though the whole time, I clench my teeth and fists while I talk about her. I was willing to do whatever I could, just like when I was a kid running away from foster homes to see her. Everything about that is totally unhealthy in every way.

I find I am struggling with this chapter as I have most of them that require a little more of me than I want to freely give. It has been about a week since I have sat in this chair to write. So much has happened in this week that I am trying to sort out in my own head. Some of it is not my story to tell, so I can't share those parts. Sometimes, I feel like I have the enemy (the devil) looking over my shoulder telling me this must stop. There is no place in this world for these words. I know he is wrong. He is wrong because the freedom that comes from healing and the love of God is good. Good comes from God, and God loves me because I am one of His children. So I continue even if it hurts or takes a little more time than planned. And it does hurt.

Sometimes, when people I care for are hurting, I feel like my heart is tearing apart for them. So the ones who get sick, I want to make you better with a hug. The ones who have atrocious things happen in your lives, I want to make it right. And yes, I want the ones who hurt you to hurt too. Those that hide because they can't talk about the pain and loneliness, I understand and I want to find you and sit with you for as long as it takes for you to face the world again. I guess what I have done all week is hide. My hiding is more from these pages, the blank spaces that need my words and punctuation. I wonder if this is how a painter feels when they look at a blank canvas.

It is just sitting there, waiting for them, for the story in their mind to be placed upon it in great expectation that the world around them will see exactly what they saw. That the feelings they so desperately want to convey will glide across the canvas with easy strokes of the brush. That's what I want, but the brush strokes are often not gentle and are rushed. Each touch of the keys can bring a tear or anger, with the goal to be healing.

All of these little rabbit trail thoughts are things I have had to face or work on in one way or the other. God isn't just working on me with my missing Mom pieces but other pieces that are bent and broken so that I can be a better mom, wife, sister, friend, aunt, Grammy, chaplain, and person. It isn't easy work, and it takes time.

When I was in active addiction, one of my sisters had to pull away from me, no contact, no reaching out at all. As she put it the other night as we talked, she couldn't reach out to me one more time and take the chance of her hand being smacked away. When I heard those words, it hit my gut pretty hard. But I get it, I really do. I used to think she was a stuck-up snob who thought she owned the world. I thought she held the world in her hands. You know the picture-perfect life. I felt like everything I did, she judged me in the worst ways, and nothing I ever did was good enough for her. I ran away from the last foster home before I turned sixteen, quit school, and got pregnant. I felt abandoned by her, just one more person to walk away because I wasn't good enough. I thought she hated me for never being able to testify against my father. I really thought she hated me.

That wasn't the case at all, and the other night I learned that truth. She was hurting for her little sister who was destroying her life. She couldn't handle the whirlpool I had jumped into and was drowning in. I should have asked if she ever thought I would get out of it. I believe she thought I would die first. Oh, heck, who am I trying to kid? I thought I was going to die before I ever had the chance to breathe the way God wanted me to. And of course, I can say that now because I had no idea what God wanted from me or who He really was. I didn't know Him; I didn't want to. I figured He hated me as much or more than I hated myself.

So how has He healed me from the missing Mom pieces? He has taken the time to show me and allow me to breathe again. Those times when I believed I was abandoned, He never left me alone. I was allowed to continue the walk I chose, yet not free from the consequences that followed.

God sent His son to die for me, to pay the price for my sin. His love for me has given me the ability to love others. I didn't do anything to deserve His love. I couldn't earn it if I tried.

> For it is by grace you have been saved, through faith—and this is not from yourselves, it is the gift of God—not by works, so that no one can boast. (Ephesians 2:8–9, NIV)

> I will exalt you, Lord, for you lifted me out of the depths and did not let my enemies gloat over me. Lord my God, I called to you for help, and you healed me. You, Lord, brought me up from the realm of the dead; you spared me from going down to the pit. Sing the praises of the Lord, you his faithful people; praise his holy name. For his anger lasts only a moment, but his favor lasts a lifetime; weeping may stay for the night, but rejoicing comes in the morning. (Psalm 30:1–5, NIV)

> So do not fear, for I am with you; do not be dismayed, for I am your God. I will strengthen you and help you; I will uphold you with my righteous right hand. (Isaiah 41:10, NIV)

God is still working on me, molding me to be who He wants me to be, needs me to be. There are times when I fight him all the way through it, mostly out of fear. When I stumble, He picks me up to continue the walk on the right path. God truly is healing my missing Mom pieces by writing it all out, writing to share with you.

He is mending my heart so the pain is not so bad, and if my heart is not hurting as much, then I can love others better. I can be there for others when they are broken and hurting.

> The Lord gave another message to Jeremiah. He said, "Go down to the potter's shop, and I will speak to you there." So I did as he told me and found the potter working at his wheel. But the jar he was making did not turn out as he had hoped, so he crushed it into a lump of clay again and started over. Then the Lord gave me this message: "O Israel, can I not do to you as this potter has done to his clay? As the clay is in the potter's hand, so are you in my hand." (Jeremiah 18:1–6, NLT)

Thank you, Lord, for not giving up on this clay pot that is cracked and needs plenty of work done on it.

Responses

1. He showed me that He is Spirit, and Spirit is not gender-based that the love that comes from Him is the mother's heart.
2. I haven't sought His healing yet because then I would have to forgive.
3. In His love and the love of my family and friends.
4. God has helped me to understand more.
5. I healed myself through self-love and reflection.
6. Him being there.
7. I learn to lay it at the Lord's feet and walk away.
8. God has provided women in my life that were "mom" figures but were younger. God also made me realize there are special things about having an older mom.
9. He loves me unconditionally.
10. She did the best she could with raising us. I understand her upbringing more now as an adult.
11. He hasn't. (3)
12. I'm a work in progress. LOL.
13. His Word and prayer.
14. With having granddaughters to show love in hugging and kisses and God's Word! And to my grandsons as well!
15. He has held me up whenever I have fallen.
16. Still working on allowing it to be healed.
17. He has walked me through forgiveness.
18. By showing me that she was working hard to give me things I needed and sometimes things I wanted.
19. He is everything I need.
20. Remembering her love.
21. Prayer. (2)
22. I'm still working on it.
23. God has healed me in more ways than anyone will ever understand.
24. Have me a mother figure.
25. I still have my father, and we talk about my mom a lot.

26. He is my strength.
27. My value was settled at the cross.
28. Brought people in to my life that help me build back my self-worth.
29. My children.
30. I'm not sure if I am healed. But going to church has allowed me to understand that everyone is full of sins and no one is perfect. I always feel terrible about the way I treated my mom because I was angry with them (my parents) for living with me when I should have been angry at my sister. I am trying to cope with it and know that my mom will forgive me.
31. I'm sure He's trying; I'm just not sure I'm ready to hear Him yet.
32. Placed people in my life to fill them.
33. Praying and guiding me to continue to have my mother be a part of my life now.
34. It has helped me knowing that He loves me and that he has a plan for me even if I didn't understand it at the time.
35. Time has healed to a point. God, not.
36. His love and promise to me. And knowing He is real, I do believe this. He has forgiven me even if I can't always forgive myself.
37. Through faith.
38. He's not done.
39. Other women have replaced them.
40. By letting me know that people do things for selfish reasons, and they usually have zero to do with me.
41. There were times when I wanted to fight the world (God), and now I deal with that feeling.
42. It's a work in progress. He's helping me set healthy, loving boundaries.
43. It's still a work in progress.
44. We're still working on that.
45. He has never left me even when I walked away from Him.
46. Giving me positive support outside of my family.

47. God's mercy. He shows it daily to me, and there have been many personal shortcomings and disappointments. But He's always there, looking out for me. I try to focus on my blessings, so maybe also perspective—my loving husband, healthy children, and our needs met, etc.

48. I have never asked Him to, never really thought about it on this level before today.

49. Peace.(2)

50. God has given me the opportunity to bring all things with her to a close.

51. I have been able to be the nonemotional child.

52. He allowed me to bring a daughter into this world.

53. Remembering her, sharing memories and time with my brothers, having two children, loving them with everything in me. And passing on her truths, love, and wisdom she gave to me.

54. I moved on from my horrible past abusive relationships and became healed. Now I'm in a healthy, loving, Godly relationship.

55. God, my church family, and my support system.

56. God has revealed that my mom loves me. That she didn't know how to handle the pressures of five kids and her own issues. The childlike longing I had to feel loved, wanted, valued, and important was so strong and can be so strong. God has reminded that my value was settled at the cross. He's softened my heart.

57. He's been helping me heal by repairing the relationship with my mother.

58. God has always been in my life. He revealed himself to me when I was sitting in a classroom in middle school. I was so in need of help, and silently, I sat there looking out the window and praying for help. All of a sudden, an over-whelming peace and mostly joy came over me. I couldn't stop smiling! I wanted to stand up and shout it out. Out the window was more beautiful a day than I had ever seen my entire life. Everything was so, so beautiful, and I knew

in my heart and soul I had been touched, my prayers were heard, and I would be okay from that moment on. Praise the Lord!

59. She is in the memories with them now. She gets to be a part of the kids' lives, and I know I can count on her to always be there for them.

60. I think, just as we both have come to know the Lord, our hearts have been healed through the years. We have always been close, and now we are much closer!

61. Showed me peace beyond understanding.

62. I have forgiven her for anything that I wish would have been different.

63. Made me forgive her, I think, so I would have healthy relationships with my husband and kids. I may never forget though.

64. God is still helping me.

65. Some, well, I can't fix her, but I know God can. It's in his hands. He knows what can help her and knows why she does the things that she does. He is in complete control.

66. God has assured me I will be with my mom in heaven again someday. The circle will be unbroken.

67. He has shown me love.

68. I have another mom who is not judgmental.

69. Open adoption.

Now it's your turn.

How has God healed you from those missing pieces?

_____
_____
_____
_____
_____
_____
_____
_____
_____
_____
_____
_____
_____
_____
_____
_____
_____
_____
_____
_____
_____
_____
_____
_____
_____
_____
_____
_____
_____

Chapter 22

What Has Happened for You to Heal from Those Missing Pieces?

I know we just had a chapter of how has God healed you. But there are people who do not know about God or believe in Him. So if they don't give Him the credit or acknowledgement, then what do they attribute their healing to? Since I know God, I have been saved through Jesus Christ; I am not going to be sharing in this chapter. This will be all about those that have responded to the questionnaires and answered this question.

Responses

1. The filling of his spirit.
2. I would have to allow myself to forgive for the healing to start.
3. Being able to share my heart and hurt with others going through similar situations and lots of prayer.
4. I've grown up. I see things different than I did before.
5. Time and giving it all to God.
6. Gave forgiveness and also forgave myself.
7. Healed.
8. A closer relationship with God and my mom.
9. I work a twelve-step program that teaches me how to live.
10. Matured and have had conversations about things.
11. She died, and I came to realize how much she had really suffered unnoticed.
12. Still healing with the help of my sisters in Christ.
13. Recognition of the need, acting on the recognition.
14. Having my own children.
15. To forgive myself.
16. Still working on it.
17. Broken heart and some powerful conversations.
18. Mostly, it was just growing up and then realizing the sacrifices that both she and my dad made for me and my sisters.
19. Jesus.
20. Waiting on God.
21. God's mercy.
22. I'm not healed. (2)
23. I have a loving family and a wonderful relationship with my church family who have all been a strong influence in my life. I have also had an endless relationship with my Lord from whom I talk daily and seek guidance from.
24. Twenty-seven years of unconditional love.
25. Time. (2)
26. Time, prayer, and reminding myself I have forgiven her.

27. Spending time with God, and Him just blessing me and showing me how much He loves me.
28. I've learned to appreciate my children more.
29. My sister and my dad filled my life with support and love, and that helped me see what I needed to work on. I give all credit to them.
30. My children.
31. I worked on myself by being a better person, standing up for myself and truly being happy.
32. Tolerance.
33. Counseling.
34. My son being in prison and my mom being a part of our lives with that whole journey.
35. Church.
36. Time and proof I am *not* my mother's child! I am a better person inside and out, and I will remain me! No one ever compares me to my mom. Her sisters agree. I am my own person and a good, kind one at that. I always put others before myself. Because I have learned what goes around comes around! I have lived long enough to see the come around and am grateful I am the way I am! I would not want to be any other way! Except maybe richer money-wise for I would do nothing but good! I try to portray exactly that.
37. Still a process, frankly. Every day gets better, some good days, some not so good. Progression and keeping strong!
38. Acceptance and knowing forgiveness.
39. I am strong and loving.
40. I've had children of my own, and I was able to provide them with my own childhood dreams.
41. I don't dwell on the past.
42. God.
43. Three years biweekly meetings with a counselor and her recommendations to go to church.
44. I'm beginning to feel peace in my upbringing.
45. Still working.

46. Soul care.
47. I'm still working on it. But mostly, talking and learning to listen to others and to be understanding and loving in things I know I need love in.
48. Some counseling but many of my reasons for the need for personal healing were due to my own mistakes and things that my mom could not control when I was a child. I've matured and sought out to understand depression, instead of condemning it.
49. I realized this isn't something I have ever healed from. These battles I still deal with today as a young mother.
50. Forgiveness.
51. I quit thinking about the things I miss about my mom.
52. It took about twenty-four years, but I finally have someone as close to me as she once was.
53. Transformed my mind like Christ.
54. Feeling wanted.
55. I became a certified peer specialist who assisted people with their heartaches, helping to heal them with talking things out and providing support.
56. I have more peace. It's definitely a work in progress, but I thank God for my mother.
57. My mom and I are getting closer as she's getting closer.
58. Years of trying to understand and forgiveness.
59. God's Holy Spirit, the Comforter, has comforted me in my loss of a great mom.
60. I go to therapy.
61. I had to get over some of the resentment I had toward her. I had to forgive her for feeling like she wasn't and wouldn't be there when I needed her.
62. The passing of my dad, our relationship with God, the miracles of life that I have seen and am a part of.
63. To show my kids all my pieces so they might not feel like they have missing pieces of me.
64. Five years ago, I turned my life around and headed down the right path.

65. Healthy new beginnings since I moved out of her house. A guy that stood up to her and said no more abuse (something I never had courage to do).
66. God blessed me with three beautiful kids, has continued to show Himself as a loving Father to me and how to love my kids.
67. Accepting that God has the power to do all things gives me a little bit of relief knowing He is in control. And telling me that I don't have to be in control of her. I don't have to play the mom of her.
68. Life.

Now it's your turn, what has happened for you to heal from those missing pieces?

_____

_____

_____

_____

_____

_____

_____

_____

_____

_____

_____

_____

_____

_____

_____

_____

_____

_____

_____

_____

_____

_____

_____

_____

_____

_____

_____

_____

_____

_____

_____

Chapter 23

If She Is Gone, What Would You Like to Say the Most to Her? Or If She Were Here and You Could Say Anything to Her, What Would It Be?

As I sit down to write this, my mother is still alive and in Texas. I figured by the time I got to this point, I could just say, well, I have said it all and there is nothing left. I apparently cannot leave it there.

There are many times I have used the word *fear* in this writing, but I wasn't sure if I was conveying exactly what that looked like to me or for me. But I had an experience that really speaks volumes as to how intense fear can be for many different reasons.

So we went to the movies one afternoon, my husband and two of the kids. As the movie started, I was eating candy, junior mints, and one got lodged in my throat. The chocolate wasn't melting fast enough and neither was the center. I started to cough but not enough to help. I got up and waved that I was fine, and I walked out of the theater. I could barely get a half-breath at a time, fear not being able to catch a full from the lungs breath. I had a fear of being alone and dying, yet not enough to cause my husband and children to panic. Fear, an emotion I am aware of, and I know it well. It often sits under the skin like another one of my natural senses. I say multiple times a day or night, faith not fear, faith not fear, and faith not fear. And then I can say thank you, God. Thank you, Jesus. The shoulders relax a bit; the heart rate slows to a steady beat, instead of erratic stomping. My eyes stop searching for the offender. I know it sounds crazy. But does it really? Don't we all fear something at one point in time or another? Maybe that's what it is, just one point in time or two or three. Maybe it's more, more intense. Maybe it's FEAR in capital letters and bold text. Do we admit it easily if it does happen? I know I am only admitting it right now because the sense of urgency was so huge at the moment, minute, minutes.

I was afraid as I stumbled into the handicap stale. I leaned over the toilet to try and cough and maybe vomit, hoping to dislodge the candy, and I couldn't do it. I stood there leaning on the wall feeling like, "Oh, crap, I should have asked John for help." I was a bit light-headed, and my ears were ringing, so I prayed. I didn't think I could make it back in there without passing out and then freaking everyone in the theater out. I literally felt trapped. Trapped that words wouldn't come out and air couldn't come in. I've known many types of fear before, but this was new. This was and is lingering a little as I share this experience with you. I find myself slowly taking a deeper breath, just to see if I can. I can. Fear passes for the moment until my throat tightens again, and my chest aches like an elephant has made it the place to sit. And I try again just to make sure I can take another breathe.

Fear: Forcibly-Excruciating-Aware-Reoccurring.

Faith: Faithfully-Anointed-Invested-Trustworthy-Healing.

Faith sounds so promising and so much sweeter. Faith not fear, my Father holds me close. His breath fills my lungs again and again and again. I exhale gently, not wanting to give up all of that breath at once. It's a battle. Faith is stronger, faith is bigger, and it is mine.

Finally, I cough one more time, and I can breathe. The candy is out! Thank you, Lord!

I cannot let fear stop me from speaking from the heart; it's a good thing to get this out. It's good not to feel like I have to be hard and that I can let my heart feel true emotion. It is okay to risk it and say now what I want her to know.

I want to pick up the phone and tell you I miss you and I have for a very long time. I would tell you that I want to bring all of the kids and grandkids over for you to meet. You have six grandchildren and twelve great grandchildren with one on the way. As well as two others that are close to our hearts. So I will change that number of great grandchildren to fourteen and one on the way! I would love to invite you to every event, every birthday party, Thanksgiving dinner, Christmas Eve, and Christmas Day. I think you would like our church very much. One of the kid's graduate college in fifteen days; it would be wonderful if you are there. It's crazy how they are all growing up and having families of their own. I don't feel as needed anymore. I know I am. I just don't hear "Mom" every five minutes anymore. When the grandchildren are around, it's Grammy every two minutes! LOL.

You're missing out on everything, Mom. You missed my first marriage, though it was nothing to cry about until the pain came. I couldn't call you; I couldn't cry for you and expect you to answer. You missed the birth of all three of my sweet baby girls, meeting my awesome stepchildren, and the adoption of a cute, little six-year-old that has turned our world upside-down a few times. You missed my second and last wedding to an amazing man! Oh, Mom, he has put up with so much from me in these twenty-four years! I spent the first twelve years sabotaging the very thing I wanted. He is my very bestest friend in the whole world. Yes, I know I said *bestest*. I like that word when it comes to him. He is loving, Mom, and patient, kind, forgiving, protective, and understanding. He has never hit me, and I have given reason, if he were that type of man. I literally begged him to just do it and get it over with one night. We were fighting because I was unfaithful. He didn't. He said he loved me, and he would never lay a hand on me to hurt me, and he hugged me. Mom, you never had that happen, did you? You don't have to worry, Mom, he loves me and takes care of me! He is a great father to all of the kids, even the kids' friends. He is a giant teddy bear, and even the littlest granddaughter knows she has him wrapped around that tiny pinky! He doesn't let anyone hurt us.

I wanted you to know that I have had a drug and alcohol problem most of my life. I started using really young, and it took a long time for me to get better. I went periods without drugs. Alcohol was legal, well, not at first. I got carded more after turning twenty-one than before. I guess the problem was I couldn't do it successfully. I have to remember that, that I couldn't do it successfully so I don't mess it up again. As of today, I have eleven years and seven months clean and sober! I'm really proud of that time; I have worked hard for it. I quit smoking cigarettes as well. That was really hard to do, but it has been fifteen years since I had one. Of course, the weight has always been an issue.

I was always so skinny as a kid. But I chunked up. I found in my life the only thing I felt I had control of was what I ate or how much or if I didn't at all. I struggled with bulimia for about six months and was tired and scared that every time I coughed, I was vomiting, and then I just did more drugs. (I can tell you the one thing I know for sure I didn't do was heroin or needles.) So then, I didn't eat at all. That's not happening now; I have gone the other direction. I really like food. I eat when I am hungry, bored, mad, sad, emotional, not emotional, and hungry. Yes, I know I said hungry twice. I said I like food. LOL.

I'm trying to be healthy. How's your health? Any more strokes, and is your diabetes under control yet? Is your deep-red hair completely gray or white yet? I get mine colored; it has been going white and gray since I was about twenty-one. Are you still painting or is that too difficult now?

Oh, and I have three tattoos. One is a cross on my leg with a face to represent Jesus on the Cross, the second is a rose and it's on my back. The third is a man and woman on my back. The man is Jesus; the woman, she is the woman at the well. She has a tear on her face because Jesus told her of the living water. She no longer needed to search for what was missing in men who didn't want the best for her. I was that woman at the well, Mom. I was always living in sin and looking for the wrong things and men to make me happy when I just needed Jesus to be alive in me!

I know we didn't go to church a lot when we were kids even though we lived right across the road from one. Did you know I used to think God hated me? I really did believe that because we went to church and I prayed and I was still being hurt. I used to wish I were dead when I was little. I couldn't tell you that because you didn't listen to anything else. I wish you would have really known Jesus then. I wish you would have run away with us and never looked back. I wish you would have fought back when he hurt us, at least try. I wish I could have saved you as he drag you through the living room by your thick red hair. I wanted to tackle him. I wanted to beat him with a bat. I wanted him dead. Every time he kicked you in the gut for crying and begging him to stop, I wanted him to die.

I'm sorry I couldn't save you from him, Mom! I'm sorry that no one helped build your self-esteem so you would have courage. You fell between the cracks of life, Mom, and no one ever noticed. I'm sorry I couldn't testify against him to get him away from you. I didn't understand that he treated you that way so he could knock your self-worth down and out. He did it to make you feel trapped and hopeless. He was successful, and I didn't realize by not testifying, I was helping him hold you down. I was a child that had no idea what putting him away really meant to all of us, especially you. I know once you said you gave us up to protect us. I only wish you could of protected yourself for us to be with us. I miss you, Mom, my heart hurts because I can't hug you. I can't laugh with you, take you to lunch, take you to appointments. I can't hug my mom, and it hurts horribly some days.

Do you miss me, Mom? Do you get sad ever because of the way life has landed us so far apart in miles and heart? It's not all your fault, Mom. I don't blame you for everything! I know life was tough, and I know the things my father would make you do. But he didn't make you walk away from me! You did that one by your own choosing, no matter what reason you had.

I am healing though, and it feels good to begin to be free. I have learned a lot about how much God loves me and all Jesus did for me. I know that through all of this pain, God has a plan for me that is so far beyond what I can fathom. Believe it or not, I am a chaplain for our church! I spend time with families that are hurting or in need of comfort at the hospital. It's hard watching families struggle, but God gets them through it all. Sometimes, it's visiting for a short time with someone in the hospital. Sometimes, it's meeting families at the ER and sitting with them for hours. I go if someone has surgery, and I hang out with the family while they wait. Sometimes, it's waiting while the loved one takes their last breath, and of course, it's the time after that too. God has called me to love and help those hurting. I believe he has placed a love in my heart and an aching in my soul for hurting people.

Mom, that's why I have done this book too. There are people like us and worse that are hurting, and I have to try and help them. They have to know that my heart hurts for them and the pain they carry. So none of this was meant to hurt you, Mom, honest. I didn't want to be in my seventies like you and have all of this pain take some of my life away every day. I don't want my girls or any of my kids to go through times of hating me. I don't want them to have the pain I have had all of my life. I want them to heal now for the pain I caused and the sin from one generation to the next that has held my ankles for so long. The chains must be cut off, Mom! I want to live, love, and walk like God wants me to. I want to be obedient to my heavenly Father!

Mom, I'm so sorry it has taken so long for me to do this. I want to call you and say it, but until you see this, you won't get it or fully understand.

Mom, I forgive you. I don't have to say it all again why, but know in my heart, I truly forgive you for all of my missing Mom pieces. I love you, always.

> Consider it pure joy, my brothers and sisters, whenever you face trials of many kinds, because you know that the testing of your faith produces perseverance. Let perseverance finish its work so that you may be mature and complete, not lacking anything. (James 1:2–4, NIV)

> Praise be to the God and Father of our Lord Jesus Christ, the Father of compassion and the God of all comfort, who comforts us in all our trouble with the comfort we ourselves receive from God. (2 Corinthians 1:3–4, NIV)

May the God of hope fill you with all joy and peace as you trust in him, so that you may overflow with hope by the power of the Holy Spirit. (Romans 15:13, NIV)

Responses

1. You are my hero.
2. What did I ever do to you for you to treat me the horrible way you did?
3. She is her, and I just want her to know she is the best and I love her so much.
4. Mom, I'm sorry for not always being the most cooperative daughter. Now that I have a daughter of my own, I understand and appreciate everything you did for me. Although we are close now, I wish we could have been more open about things when I was younger, but that doesn't mean I didn't have a good childhood. You always did what was best for me, and I hope that I will be as good of a role model for my daughter as you have been for me.
5. I love you. (4)
6. I understand the way you are, but that doesn't mean I approve.
7. I love you! I miss you! And I'd ask for one more hug!
8. I forgive you for not always being there for me.
9. I would tell her how thankful I am that she raised me, put up with me, and was such an incredible example of mercy and grace for me!
10. Thank you for what you taught me and you love me.
11. She's still alive. I never miss the chance to tell her that *I love her* and how much she means to me.
12. I love her just the way she is.
13. I appreciate you every day.
14. I'm sorry, and I miss you more than I could have dreamed I would.
15. I have become the person I am because of you.
16. I love you. and I'm so happy you were my mom.
17. How about these grandkids!?
18. That I love her and understand she is broken.
19. I love you, Mama.

20. Look at me now! You knew I would make it, didn't ya!? Thank you for praying over me!
21. Thank you for being you.
22. That I love you very much, you are so much more than a mother to me. You are my mommasita, friend, and think tank. If we were allowed to choose our mother, I would choose you again and again. I love you, Mom.
23. That I am proud of her.
24. She did a good job.
25. Love you much.
26. I wish I'd been more thoughtful.
27. Please know your words had the power to tear me down completely, but they also had the power to cause me to soar to new heights. I love you, and I know you tried your best. I appreciate your sacrifice.
28. I love you, and I understand.
29. I keep wanting to ask her if she knows Christ as her personal savior because I can't imagine a heaven without her.
30. Thank you.
31. Thank you for showing me the power of unconditional love.
32. Thank you, Mom, for everything and please keep looking down upon us and smile. We are doing the best we can without you.
33. I wanted you to know my kids.
34. You have taught me to be a kind, loving, and giving person.
35. I love you more than you could ever know.
36. Thank you for being my mom.
37. I miss you.
38. I love you and thank you for tolerating my teenage years.
39. She's gone. That there is not a day that goes by that I don't still need and wish she was here.
40. You destroyed me as a person.
41. I'm thankful for her sacrifice all these years, saving up to pay for all of our college tuition. I'm grateful that she loves and spoils my kids so much.

42. My mom passed away almost four years ago. I miss her so much. If she was still here, I would tell her I love and miss her.
43. I wish I had told you I love you more often.
44. That she means the world to me, but that words could never express how I feel.
45. Take responsibility for what you have done. Apologize, it wasn't my fault. I was not a bad child all of the time, but you were the adult. I didn't deserve your beatings.
46. I know it's not my fault you left. And I'm no longer mad at you.
47. I wish I would have kept in touch with her more over the years.
48. I loved you in a strange way, a lot like the way you loved me I think. Just wish others did not come before us! *Stop* worrying what the neighbors think! Stop trying to keep up with the Jonses and be real! Don't sweat the small stuff!
49. She is luckily still here. Thank you, Lord, for that! She's not well, had not been for years, so I try as much to visit and call. I want her to know she's so important, not just a little but extremely. She gave me room to mess up in life but also reap the harsh consequences. Mom, I can't imagine the day you will no longer be here, I can't and I won't. It is hard to think that you were strong for us kids, and you always did everything on your own. When your family mistreated you (they will have to answer to God for that), when my bio dad hurt you and all of us, you pushed on, and I have nothing bad to say. I am sorry for being a jerk later in my teenage years. I'm sorry I got married at seventeen and moved far away. I'm sorry I let you down so many times. Sorry can never begin to explain it. But the Lord has blessed me with you, and now we are close. You're one of my rocks that I could never live without, and I love you so much, Mom. You did an amazing job with what you had. I will forever be grateful for a mother like you.
50. How do I keep going? Am I good enough?

51. You taught me how to live a wonderful life and raise wonderful children.
52. I don't understand her.
53. Why when I was younger, did you make me feel like I wasn't ever good enough?
54. I would tell her how much I love and miss her.
55. Why couldn't you be as kind to me as you were fake to others?
56. Love you, Mom. What do you need? Let me help.
57. Thank you for loving me enough to give me two moms when everyone would have understood if you decided to hate each other instead.
58. I would talk with her about Christ.
59. I love you and miss you so much. And I want to thank you and Daddy for being so strict.
60. I forgive you. (2)
61. Mom, so sorry for all the heartache I've caused you over the years being rebellious as I was. I love you!
62. She is gone. But I would tell her that I am still serving the Lord and that I will see her soon.
63. That I love you and respect you. You mean everything to me.
64. I love you and appreciate everything you do.
65. I hope you know how loved you are every day of your life.
66. Thank you for making me as strong and stubborn as you did. And for giving me a soft heart to love others with. Thank you for allowing me to grow and be independent even though I know it was hard for you.
67. I'm sorry.
68. Let go of the hurt and live your best life. Resolve it. Get the help that you need, love yourself a little. God forgave you, now it's time to forgive yourself. Don't let your past mistakes and depression swallow up your days.
69. Thank you.
70. I love you and I miss you, but I'm glad you no longer hurt.

71. She is terminally ill now. I want her to know how loved she is, that she was an amazing mother. And I am so grateful God chose her to be my mother. Also, I want her to know I will always carry her in my heart.
72. Wish things could have been different.
73. Thank you for making me the woman I am today!
74. Mostly, I just want her to know how much I miss her influence and wisdom and how much it hurts that I never go to see her interact with my daughter, her granddaughter.
75. Thank you for being such a wonderful mom, for loving me so much, and for instilling your wisdom of the power of God and faith in Christ. Oh, and how do I thread the bobbin on your sewing machine? I can't figure it out for the life of me. (I know it seems insignificant, but the struggle is real!)
76. Why didn't you show my sisters and I what a healthy relationship was so we didn't fall into the trap? I love you, even though we never heard it.
77. I love to hear you voice and feel your hugs.
78. Mom, I love and miss you so much. *I hate ALS.*
79. I would say I love you, Mom. I forgive you. I know you did the best you could. I wish mental illness was something that was understood more at the time. I wish your own mental issues would have been addressed and then you may have been able to help me with my mental illness.
80. I love her to the moon and back, and I wish I had more time.
81. Why am I less important?
82. I am glad that we have gotten close again and glad to have her back in my life. It's nice to be able to call my mom again just because.
83. Thanks for being the best mom ever, for your love and never giving up on me! Thanks for being my friend.
84. She went home June 8, 2008 and if she were here, I would ask her more questions about my dad.

85. Thank you for everything you have done for me and my kids. You have helped me every time I needed anything. I love you!
86. That even how she treated me back then I still love her.
87. Thank you, Grandma, you were such an example of unconditional love and acceptance. You showed me the love of the Father and an example to follow.
88. Mom, please ask for help, and when someone offers help, please take it. Don't let yourself go take pride in things you do. Go do something for yourself to be happy. Take a break from things that are stressing you out. I want you to be happy and be able to relax a bit and not worry about everyone and everything all the time.
89. Mom is in heaven. I'd tell her I love her so much! I am so thankful for her. I wish I had done more for her.
90. Why didn't you believe me when I told you what happened to me?
91. I would tell her I know we don't see eye to eye all the time but I love you.
92. Thanks for putting up with me.
93. Thank you for giving me a chance. You regret your decision often, but had you changed your mind, neither of us would be here today.

Now it's your turn.

If she is gone, what would you like to say the most to her? Or if she were here and you could say anything to her, what would it be?

_____

_____

_____

_____

_____

_____

_____

_____

_____

_____

_____

_____

_____

_____

_____

_____

_____

_____

_____

_____

_____

_____

_____

_____

Chapter 24

Would You Like to Write a Small Paragraph as a Tribute to Your Mother?

Rose, you have always been in my heart, and I know that you always will be. Thank you for giving me the chance to have a life and a family. Thank you for showing me a tiny piece of you that was sweet and loving. I thank you for all of my sisters and brothers, though we don't always see things the same, I love them all dearly. Even though it was hard when you walked away, I got to have the chance to experience life outside of what you knew and experienced. Thank you for loving me the best way you knew how. Thank you for being my first mom. The one who held me first, picked me up when I cried, and loved me first. I may have been your fourth child, but you were my first mom! May God bless you with your remaining days by removing your guilt and pain and filling your heart and soul with his deep love for you and allow his light to shine like a beacon in a lighthouse. May it be bright and full of life until the day he takes you home. And if we do not meet again here on earth, I can only imagine how wonderful it will be to meet you in heaven with Jesus! God bless you, Mom. And since tomorrow is Mother's day, Happy Mother's day. I love you/

Always, without pain or regrets,

Christy Lynn

Responses

1. Mom, thank you for taking care of my children when I was not able to. Your love, care, and nurturing to them provided them with stability that they desperately needed. That stability has been foundational for them.

2. Mom, thank you for being my mom. God knew just the right people to have raise this child. Thank you for reading me Bible stories while I ate my cheerios. Thank you for finger paints and sharing your big roll of paper to draw on. Thank you for teaching me to sing "Away in a Manger" and a hundred Christmas program recitations and even more Bible verses and about Jesus, my Savior. Thanks for picking me up every Friday so I didn't have to stay at college alone. Thank you for taking me to five or six stores in at least three different towns to find just the right wedding dress. Thank you for helping me pack up my stuff and move from your house to our trailer and from our trailer to our new house and from that house to our home on the farm. Thanks for talking to me and keeping me alert on tired drives home from work. Thank you for praying for me, my husband, for our foster son, for our jobs, for our safety, for our happiness. Most of all, thank you for all the love a kid could ever want or need and more. I love you too.

3. She was fun to be around. We were two peas in a pod, had the same styles. Even if we were mad at each other, we could still talk to each other. She didn't always like sitting around, so we'd go shopping or just drive around. Loved being in the kitchen with her, helping her cook or bake. She always encouraged me no matter what! She was my best friend! We loved some of the same movies. Loved hiking or just being outside, just being together. We had Monday night dinners with my parents. She was very happy when I told her I started going to church again. Even took her a few times before she passed away.

4. Mommy, you are a woman that truly fears the Lord and Savior. Your gentleness pushes me to respond in love and always contemplate how my words will affect others. Thank you for always urging me to look at the world through the lens Scripture. You are a strong and courage-filled wife and mother, and I am so grateful the Lord has given me you.

5. She is no longer with us but she taught me how to love a child that is not yours biologically.

6. My mom has persevered through more than I can imagine. She carries herself with strength and dignity that can only be from God. I am beyond grateful that she is a part of my everyday life.

7. My mom, my friend, my confidant, my role model. How different I might be if not for her. She has been the one to help fill the missing pieces in my heart and has been there always in the most difficult times of my life. I have seen *her* go through difficult times with unwavering faith, strength, and perseverance. When I asked her one time how she dealt with it all, she replied she prays every day. I can only aspire to be like her and try to always remember to tell her how much I love her.

8. Like I said, my mother is the strongest person I know. She raised seven children on her own, the oldest being sixteen and the youngest two. And never once gave up on us. She cleaned houses and any other odd jobs she could find. But she kept us together as a family.

9. Emma, Geraldine Beistel Raymond, my wonderful mother. I couldn't have hand picked a better one. You taught me so much and loved me unconditionally. I think of you each and every day. I love and miss you so much, but I have peace knowing that one day we will be together again.

10. Mom, you were an amazing mother as you taught me to be a hard worker in all I did! Thank you for showing me Jesus! I miss your laughter, your bright eyes, your devotion to our family, and how you held us together! When you passed, all was gone! Nothing held together in the family! Gone! Just

Gone! You would be proud how you shine through me as a mother and a grandmother with your grandchildren and great grandchildren! You are mentioned often, and many times, I use the phrase "I just did a Priscilla there!" Thank you mom for being my mother and for loving God with all you heart! We will be together again someday in glory and praise our Lord together as we sit at His merciful feet! Love you, Mom! Lovey love and two hand wave! Your Karen Pearl.

11. All I really can say is thank you for being who God made you to be, my mother.

12. Mom, you didn't have the best marriage, but through it all, you kept us safe, and we felt your love always. You have given us everything you could, but the best thing you gave me was your time and unconditional love. You made us strong, loving, independent women. I thank you for being my mom.

13. My mom has always been one of my biggest fans. She often put herself down but always made me feel like I could do anything. She truly loves me unconditionally and never said "I told you so" when I made choices that she warned me about. My mom is truly my best friend, and I am so blessed to be her daughter.

14. My mom had me at eighteen and my sister shortly after. Young and without much help, she did everything she could to love and care for us. When she married again and had my two brothers, she had to again work to support us. She always worked hard and was often tired but loving us was always top priority. None of us are perfect, but love truly covers other shortcomings. Very glad she taught me that truth. Just wish she knew my Jesus!

15. If only more could have known you.

16. To my biological mother, I love you! I know you cared for me and tried your hardest. Thank you for loving me the best way that you can, for giving birth to me even at a very young age, and for keeping me even though I made

your life more complicated. Your love and actions did not go unnoticed! I know you look back now and think you could have done things better and sometimes get sad about some of the choices you made, but don't dwell on it. I still love you! For my grandma, thank you for making sure all my needs were met. I came first. I felt safe with you. I still do! I never felt fearful or unsure when with you. I know I was loved even when you didn't say it because your actions spoke so loudly! There is love in your hugs, conversation, and your home-cooked meals!

17. Thank you, God, for giving me the greatest mom in the world for me. Because of her, I am the woman I am today. I love you, Annabel Walker Owens!

18. A mother's job is never easy, and most mothers try to do the best they know how to do. I believe my mom did. The truth is, we never fully understand all that until we become mothers ourselves. And then we make our own mistakes.

19. Mom, there is not a day that goes by that I do not regret being there for you in the end. But I have never forgiven myself for it, and I know that you more than likely have. But you were the best mother I could ask for. I loved you then, I love you now. There will be a time I see you soon. Love forever, Billie.

20. I wish I had appreciated her more as she was an angel on earth. She kept her sense of humor and compassion and forgiveness through more adversity than most people ever experience.

21. My mom has always done the best for me. I know moms aren't supposed to have a favorite, but she always told me I was hers, and she loves my brown eyes. Words will never express the love I have for my mom.

22. Mom, what can I say? You are a huge part of me. I can sometimes look in the mirror and see you smiling back. When I'm having a bad day, I call and talk to you. I enjoy our talks and the things we say others would say we are crazy! Maybe, we are. But nothing or no one can and will

ever take your place. I love you for everything you did for me growing up, and you never gave up on me. And I will never give up on you. As the years go on, I know how very blessed I am to still have you in my life, and others say they have the best mom? But have they met my mother? I love you, JJB, you're always number one in my eyes. My mother, father, and friend all in one, I hope you know how much you are loved.

23. I would not be the person I am today without her. I only wish I would have been able to show her more of the love that she showed me before she was called home. But I have faith that she knows.

24. Mom, you taught me how to be wise beyond my years. How to forgive when I didn't think I could. And how to love with everything I have, and to always help those in need, no matter how small the gesture.

25. Mom died when I was twenty. I would like to say to my mom, let's go out for lunch and shopping. Get to know her as a friend and let her know I became a woman that loves her so much. I'm sorry for being a bratty teenager.

26. My mom!

27. I was so lucky to be born in 1953 when life was much simpler, and I was also lucky to have great Christian, God-fearing parents who raised me and my sisters and brothers to be the same. I often thought they were too strict when I was young but realized later in life that they did it right. I am thankful for all the lickings (paddling's) I got, and I'm glad for all I've given my girls because they turned out to be wonderful parents themselves.

28. When people ask who your hero is, the go-to answer is often parents. Most people say this like a machine, but for me, it's always been 100 percent authentic. My mother has shaped me into the woman I am today. There are many days she went without, just so I had what I needed. She went to work on days that she should have stayed home; she was a provider. When I had a cancerous tumor removed, she was

my rock. If I am half the woman she is when I have children, I will consider myself blessed. They say that as you grow up, your mother becomes your best friend. I am not sure who "they" are, but boy are they right.

29. My mom has been such a great role model. She has always been there in times of need. And when you really don't know what to do, she is always there to talk to you and help in any way she can. She is a loving person and a very honest person.

30. Mom, you're beautiful, kind, smart, and always knows what to say. You have helped me to grow in my faith and education. I owe you the world. I love you more.

31. To a woman who has given unending love to so many people. Thank you for your gentleness and support. My life would be incomplete without you.

32. Peggy June is alive in our hearts. She sits at the right hand of God and waits for us there.

33. I love you, Mom, even though we didn't have much time together. I've learned what I need and what I do not need or want in my life.

34. Ellen Black, your love and compassion means so much to me.

35. My mother was the most awesome person, from cooking, cleaning, canning, and candy/ cookie making to putting up/repairing fencing on our farm, feeding cattle and pigs to putting pigs in a "maternity ward," and watching over them as they gave birth. My mother was an all-around doer, a nurturer, and the love of my dad's life for fifty-and-a-half years. She had so much faith. I love and miss her so much.

36. Mom, I love you so much. I wish I would have appreciated your silliness more. But it's something I treasure. We've been around and around and through so much together. You've been my best friend and loyal confidante. We grew up together, didn't we? You are so passionate about our family. As a child, I was stifling, now that I have healthy boundaries in place, I appreciate your fierceness. I know you want me to be happy and healthy. I'm working on it.

It's hard to believe you're seventy. That was an eye opener for me when I realized you weren't going to be here forever. I don't want you to die without knowing I'm okay and that what I feel for you is love. I don't want to have regrets, and you've lived that way your whole life.

37. Dear Mom, I know we have had a troubled relationship over the years, but as I've grown, I've seen the struggles you've gone through to raise me. I'm sorry for that hurt I've caused. You are now my best friend. I'm proud to call you my mother, my mom.

38. Mom, I now see it was the best you could do. By the grace of God, I've received everything you couldn't manage yourself. Love, Me.

39. Oh wow, my mom. She's been my best friend, my rock, my singing partner, my late night trips to Wal-Mart buddy, and at times, she was someone I thought I hated more than anyone. But now, after years of the on-and-off relationship with my mother, I am more grateful for her than I have ever been. She has taught me a lot in life, and something she probably doesn't realize. I don't think my mom was ever a "bad" mom. I know she always did her best, and sometimes, her depression just didn't allow it. But I've definitely learned what I think is going to help me be the best mom I could be. And I really do have her to thank for that. I hope that one day, my kids can experience that late night dance parties in the living room with their friends and myself that my friends and I grew to love every weekend. Thank you, Mom, for all the good and the bad. Thank you for loving not only Quincy and Kenzie but also loving Dre, Jada, and Kirstyn as well. That four years have been challenging, but thank God, it's frowned upon for humans to eat their children, ha-ha! I love you, Mom! Love, Bratsy.

40. My mom, a child, a sister, an aunt, gram, great-grandmother, and most of all, my friend, Glenda L. Guyer. I love you with all my heart. I was not always a good son in my eyes, but in her eyes, I will always be her baby boy!

41. Mom, you were a very good mother to me and my two sisters. I now come to realize that your strength and wisdom only came from the great love you had for God. You showed me to always look for the good in people and to love and encourage young people. You never said anything bad about all your friends. I've seen many times, you were knocked down by life, but you always came back strong. And the weekend that you passed, I know, you looked at me with a smile that you knew you were going home very soon, and you did. You and Jesus branded that smile I will hold till I come home too. Love and miss you, Ricky. I would call my mom every day for years, and when she went to heaven, it took a long time to get used to not calling to chat with her.

42. I wish you would have taught me about the more important things in life, instead of letting me make my own mistakes over and over again. I know people learn from making their own mistakes, but many of them could have been avoided. I don't blame my mom for any mistakes I made in life. I love her and would do anything for her, and I wish she could find happiness and joy in her life again.

43. My mom totally blessed me and my family. Mom gave me unconditional love and was always proud of our accomplishments and the grandchildren's accomplishments. Mom was a special gift from God all my life! Even as mom suffered and died from congestive heart failure, she never complained and always loved all of us.

44. I know this book has been a very difficult journey for you. But you kept pushing through it. You've taken risks and put yourself out there on so many levels, and I'm so proud of you. Nobody is perfect, and you have been more than willing to admit that about yourself, especially when it came to writing this book. That takes so much courage, and I respect you so much for that. I love you!

45. Mom, thanks for loving me and my babies with all your heart. Thank you for giving me a chance at life, a life I

hope I can give my kids too. We may not have always seen eye-to-eye, but your wisdom has always guided me, even if I did not let it be known. Love you.

46. Mom, you made the hardest, most selfless choice a mother could make. But you gave us both our lives when you made your decision. You wouldn't be here today if you hadn't. Thank you for sharing your experiences, wisdom, and grace with me. I'm so happy I get to have you in my life. I love telling people I have two moms.

Now it's your turn.

Would you like to write a tribute to your mother?

_____
_____
_____
_____
_____
_____
_____
_____
_____
_____
_____
_____
_____
_____
_____
_____
_____
_____
_____
_____
_____
_____
_____
_____
_____
_____
_____
_____
_____
_____

This has been a tough yet amazing journey, and I thank you for going on it with me. I could not have done any of this without having a relationship with Jesus Christ! If you feel that tug at your heart, if you know that you are missing something besides mom pieces, will you ask yourself if you truly know Jesus? Has he been invited into your life as your Savior? Have you thought I know I have sinned, and I can't do it anymore on my own?

If you have felt this or are feeling this way, won't you cry out to Him? Some may say you have to say a certain prayer, but it's easier than that. It is you simply crying out to Jesus, talk to Him, and tell Him how you need Him. Tell Him how you need to be different. Just have a conversation with Him. Will you invite Jesus into your heart and life today?

And if you choose salvation, this adoption in to God's family as His child, will you reach out to someone? Will you tell them what life change you have made so they can guide you further and into a deeper relationship with Him? Will you find someone who loves Jesus too and learn about His love for you?

Before I go, I want to leave you with a few more things. I was at an event today, and we did an activity that I had forgotten about from a while ago. Too many times, all we hear are the negative and the lies the enemy wants us to believe. He wants us to hang on to these lies to stop us from being a vessel God can use to bring light to the world. The enemy doesn't care about our yesterdays or our past because it's already happened. But we can be reminded of all the things we did or were told to make us think God can't possibly use our messed up pasts to further the kingdom. It can be lies we tell ourselves, things people have said about us, the choices we made or things that happened that can hold us back. I wonder if any of you can relate to that. So let's lay those lies down, let's expose them for what they are, lies. You may be being told lies that I don't mention. If so, will you lay it down as well? Will you throw it at the enemy and let him keep them? There is a reason for this. We will throw the lies back at the enemy, and we will pick up the truths that God has for us!

Ugly fat not worthy
Just a statistic
Afraid you never finish anything
Not tall not seen
Wanted too skinny
Lies, not a good parent
You're a waste of time
Dumb, I should have known better
You're a mistake, weak
Stupid lazy
If only . . .
I should be more like . . .
Invisible unqualified
You're not worth it
It's my fault not loved
failure not good enough
God can't and won't use you for good.

Authentic, valued, you are
Truths, loved
You are uniquely beautiful
Desired
Hand-picked powerful
God sees you
You are wanted
Talented
Not alone, created with a purpose
Strong, you are needed
A masterpiece
One of a kind, forgiven
Healed
Significant, whole
Overcomer
You are enough, courageous
Called by God for great things!!!!

If you want to share your story, if you need prayer for or you want to share your thoughts on this book, I would love to hear from you. Thank you for spending time with me. (Cfoxlaw72mompieces@gmail.com)

Do you or someone you know need help, someone to talk to? *Please don't wait, reach out today!*

National Domestic Violence Hotline

\# 1-800-799-SAFE (7233)
National Sexual Abuse Hotline
\# 1-800-656-4673
National Suicide Hotline
\# 1-800-273-TALK (8255)

Let's plant some seeds:

> And if I go and prepare a place for you, I will come back and take you to be with me that you also may be where I am. (John 14:3)

> For we must all appear before the judgment seat of Christ, that each on may receive what is due him for things done while in the body, whether good or bad. (1 Corinthians 15:10)

Do I believe that we will give an account for every seed?
Yes, I do!

Standing in the very presence of Jesus with a full receptacle of seeds Is *not* a good plan. The seed, the treasure is for now, *not* later!

> Bear with each other and forgive whatever grievances you may have against one another. (Colossians 3:13) (*forgiveness*)
> Seeds continue . . .

But encourage one another daily. (Hebrews 3:13) (*encouragement*)

And let us consider how we may spur one another on toward love and good deeds. (Hebrews 10:24) (*spurring one another on*)

Share with God's people who are in need. Practice hospitality. (Romans 12:13) (*meet someone's needs*)

Bless those who persecute you; bless and do not curse. (Romans 12:14) (*bless*)

Impress them on your children. Talk about them when you sit at home and when you walk along the road, when you lie down and when you get up. (Deuteronomy 6:7) (*teach*)
     Seeds continue . . .

Rejoice with those who rejoice; mourn with those who mourn. (Romans 12:15) (*help carry their burden or celebrate*)

Help the weak, be patient with everyone. (1 Thessalonians 5:14) (*patience with others*)

However, each one of you also must love his wife as he loves himself, and the wife must respect her husband. (Ephesians 5:33) (*respect spouse*)

Snatch others from the fire and save them . . . (Jude 1:23) (*share the gospel, Jesus's love*)

"Go, stand in the temple courts," he said, "and tell the people the full message of this new life." (Acts 5:20) (*tell of this new life*)
      Closing prayer:

Father God, we have done it! We have walked on this path together with great expectation of how you will use it to touch other lives. May the readers see you, how you heal, love and care for your children. I pray they see this mighty loving Father that just wants to hold His children and breathe life in to them. If you are reading this, we are speaking to you. Will you call out to Jesus, will you tell Him what you are going through and that you need Him? Will you allow Him to enter your wounded heart? Will you give your hurts, pains, and troubles to Him? Will you give Him a chance to show you a peace that will make absolutely no sense in times of struggles or crisis? A peace beyond your understanding, will you grab a hold of that? Will you allow joy to replace the fractured parts of your life? Will you allow yourself to take one more chance on a loving relationship that won't hurt you, won't let you down or walk away from you? Will you cry out to Jesus and ask Him to be the Savior of your life? It's okay to hit your knees and cry out. He is waiting on you to invite Him in!
      In Jesus's name, I pray, Amen!

Acknowledgments

I want to give my love and thanks to my amazing husband, John, for always being my biggest encourager in life. John, you are amazing, and I thank you for putting up with my baggage of frustration all these years. I thank you for standing up for me when you could have taken the easy way out. I thank you for standing with me as God moved both of us together on a path closer to him! I love you!

Thank you to all of our kids and all who have called me Mom. I love all of you, and I know it wasn't always easy. To Brittany, Katie, and Amanda, I know being my daughters has not always been a cake walk, but you have walked it well. No matter how much we are alike, in looks, attitude, passion for our families, you are still your own person. Grab ahold of who God has created you to be so you can make a path your very own. Be the best you that God gave you breath to be, and that actually goes for all of "my kids!" May you always know, never doubt for even a second, that I love you!

My big *sis*, you are my hero, and I love you. Don't quit fighting for who you are, don't forget God loves you. To our biggest *sis*, it's okay to heal! You don't have to carry this pain and guilt around anymore, it's not yours to hang on to. I love you.

My bio family, I pray when the Holy Spirit tugs at your heart, you let Jesus come in. Those that know Jesus, let Him move in your life. Move closer to Him.

My sisters and brothers in Christ, thank you for prayers and encouragement. Thank you for being there when it seemed so dark at times in our family. And for being there to celebrate as we walked closer to God with joy in our hearts! Special love to those that prayed for this journey, that listened to the constant talk of the book, that helped me get it out there for the questionnaires to be seen and done, and for the idea of actually taking the step to start writing it. What a godly family to be blessed with!

Thank you so much, God, for all you have done in my life! You loved me, and Jesus saved me from eternal pain and the pain I have lived, and the Holy Spirit moves in me to walk closer to You! I know I am blessed beyond my understanding, Father! May You be the one that receives all honor and glory for this project! Thank You for moving my heart to show the love You have to give all of us!

Christy Lynn Fox-Lawler

About the Author

Christy Lawler is a mother, a chaplain, and works with her husband, John, of nineteen years in the church wood ministry. If she is not cutting wood or going on hospital visits, she is spending time with her children and grandchildren. It was not always this way. She is a recovering drug addict and alcoholic. She has struggled with depression, anxiety, and other issues throughout her childhood and adult life. In 2007, she was saved and became a Christian by asking Jesus into her heart and life. That is why *Missing Mom Pieces* was written so others out there would know they are not alone and that someone gets it and also to give hope to those who have struggled with life issues and desired healing.

9 781644 168882